WELFARE REFORM

Failure & Remedies

Alvin L. Schorr

Foreword by Herbert J. Gans

PRAEGER

Westport, Connecticut
London

Library of Congress Cataloging-in-Publication Data

Schorr, Alvin Louis, 1921–
    Welfare reform : failure & remedies / Alvin L. Schorr ; foreword by
Herbert J. Gans.
      p. cm.
    Includes bibliographical references and index.
    ISBN 0–275–97064–7 (alk. paper)—ISBN 0–275–97065–5 (pbk. : alk. paper)
    1. Public welfare—United States. 2. Welfare recipients—Employment—
United States. 3. Poor—United States. 4. United States—Social policy—
1993– I. Title.
HV91.S2944   2001
361.973—dc21   00–052424

British Library Cataloguing in Publication Data is available.

Library of Congress Catalog Card Number: 00–052424
ISBN: 0–275–97064–7
    0–275–97065–5 (pbk.)

First published in 2001

Praeger Publishers, 88 Post Road West, Westport, CT 06881
An imprint of Greenwood Publishing Group, Inc.
www.praeger.com

Printed in the United States of America

The paper used in this book complies with the
Permanent Paper Standard issued by the National
Information Standards Organization (Z39.48–1984).

10 9 8 7 6 5 4 3 2 1

To Ann, my love

The Irish potato famine of the 1840s killed well over a million people and led as many more to emigrate to the United States. In dealing with the famine, the British government was moved, Cecil Woodham-Smith wrote, by parsimony,

but obtuseness, short-sightedness and ignorance probably contributed more . . . Much of this obtuseness sprang from the fanatical faith of mid-nineteenth century British politicians in the economic doctrine of laissez faire, no interference by government, no meddling with the operating of natural causes. Adherence to laissez faire was carried to such a length that in the midst of all of the major famines of history, the government was perpetually nervous of being too good to Ireland and of corrupting the Irish people by kindness, and so stifling the virtues of self reliance and industry. . . .

The famine left hatred behind. Between Ireland and England the memory of what was done and endured has lain like a sword.

The Great Hunger, Ireland, 1845–1849
Cecil Woodham-Smith

Contents

Foreword

Alvin Schorr's *Welfare Reform: Failure & Remedies* is the best general book I have read on welfare and welfare reform. And well it might be, for the author is not only a dean of social policy analysts but a social worker as well. He was also the dean of New York University's School of Social Work and deputy assistant secretary in the federal department of Health, Education, and Welfare when Lyndon Johnson was president.

Concise, easy to read at all times, with 45 tables of statistics for those wanting more, the book lays out the whole story of welfare from its origins to its future. Schorr begins with the start of the program as an inferior form of social security for the poor, and then charts its growth into a very minimal income support program for the victims of rural industrialization and urban deindustrialization.

For a short period in the latter half of the 1960s, the country was generous enough—and/or upset by the ghetto disorders in many big cities—to increase welfare benefits. These good old days did not last long, however. The Vietnam War and the arrival of Richard Nixon in the White House began a long, steady decline of welfare that has culminated, a quarter century later, in Bill Clinton's promise to end welfare as we knew it, giving the Republicans the opportunity to end it altogether.

The rest of Schorr's book describes the welfare "reform" that now requires poor people to work, but in badly paying and often temporary jobs. Schorr also reports the results of the early studies that describe what reform is doing for and to the poor. Like almost all federal programs, the new one helps those most who are most likely to succeed, that is, helps those who need help least, and thus looks more successful than it actually is.

As the author points out, most former welfare recipients have a sadder story to tell, particularly because they are treated as not deserving of the human rights most of us take for granted. Too many workers lose their jobs when a child gets sick and they have to take a day or two off from work. Also, many of the more fortunate still end up with an income lower than they received with welfare. In addition, they may be deprived of the food stamps and Medicaid to which they continue to be entitled under the law.

Schorr also describes the illogic underlying welfare reform. For example, government policies once reinforced that part of the American dream about the desirability of mothers, and now sometimes even fathers, to stay home with their babies and young children. Then, reforms came along, explicitly denying poor mothers this option and forcing them to go to work. Some ex-recipients wind up with jobs caring for the children of affluent mothers while their own children have to get along without their mothers.

There is a surfeit of heartlessness in welfare reform; as always, poor people get poor services. Recipients are harassed with new rules, typically administered with pitiless rigor by officials and clerks who are almost uniformly hostile toward their clients. Every possible obstacle is put in the way of the poor; even those trying to pull themselves up by their own bootstraps are often kicked down again. Sometimes it would appear as if the government is trying to prevent the survival of the most vulnerable ex-recipients.

No one knows what will happen next, especially if and when full employment ends. Because the former welfare recipients were often the last workers to be hired, they are apt to be the first fired. Then, Schorr suggests, welfare of some sort will have to be reinvented, although not under that name, and he ends the book by outlining what should be done.

Schorr argues that the work-centered concept of welfare reform should continue, pointing out that Americans, including welfare recipients, have long rejected the notion of people staying home at the expense of taxpayers. Schorr urges a sweeping series of economic reforms including higher low- and moderate-level wages and a larger role for the Earned Income Tax Credit or a Child Tax Credit.

When food stamps, Medicaid, and supports from other federal programs, especially for children, are added, a more humane replacement for welfare and welfare reform may emerge. Still, any new program also has to provide public jobs for those who cannot find jobs and income supports in lieu of welfare for those who are unable to work.

Whether enough political support can be cobbled together on behalf of a less-punitive successor to welfare reform may depend on whether willing urban and suburban politicians can sell such a program to their constituents. That, in turn, could depend on whether urban and suburban taxpayers are sufficiently horrified if and when more poor mothers with small children begin to live on the streets, begging or selling themselves to feed their families. Race is, as always, a crucial factor, for the taxpayers are mostly white, and the homeless mothers often black and Hispanic.

As a number of observers have pointed out, America provides socialism for the rich, with the corporate welfare, tax benefits, and other subsidies that their power enables them to obtain. Capitalism is reserved for the poor, requiring them to compete against each other for unskilled jobs, affordable nonslum housing, and other limited resources.

Actually, the treatment of the poor is too often a throwback to 19th century capitalism, aiming only toward the survival of the fittest. Welfare reform is a telling example of this offensive principle, but Schorr is an optimist, and his hopefulness about future antipoverty policy gives the book an almost happy ending.

Herbert J. Gans
Robert S. Lynd Professor of
Sociology, Columbia University
Author, *The War Against the Poor*

Acknowledgments

Many people have helped in the development of this small book, primarily by commenting on drafts of material but also by discussing issues, offering support (if not rudely pressing me to get finished), and providing necessary bits of information. I mention first of all my wife, Ann, and my children, Jessica, Kenneth, and Wendy—each of whom is expert on some of these matters. It is appropriate, too, to mention my grandchildren, Kafia, Eddie, Talia, Lily, and Jeremy, whose world as adults has been much in my mind as I wrote this.

Others to thank are Robert A. Levine, Jared Bernstein, Herbert J. Gans, Marvin E. Frankel, Marvin Feldstein, Martha Ozawa, Blanche Coll, Cynthia Miller, Eric R. Kingson, Sue Pearlmutter, Max B. Sawicky, Diana Tittle, and Barney Opperman.

Three disaster-relief people in a computer office at Case Western Reserve University, Sharon Scinicariello, Margaret Cooney, and Jared Bendis, devoted countless hours on the telephone to help keep my word processor in line or online. Without their skill and extraordinarily patient help, I would have lost my mind before I could complete the book.

Finally, I should acknowledge the willing and efficient help of Jill Norton in assembling the tables in the Appendix and the support of the George Gund Foundation and the Federation for Community Planning for research assistance. I am grateful to all.

A number of these people made suggestions and offered corrections, but I alone am responsible for any errors that remain.

I gratefully acknowledge permission to use material from a chapter that I contributed to a book edited by John E. Hansan and Robert Morris, *Welfare Reform, 1996–2000—Is There a Safety Net?* in 1999 by Auburn House, an imprint of Greenwood Publishing Group. This material is used in Chapter 5.

Also, permission to reproduce tables from *Shifting Fortunes: The Perils of the Growing American Wealth Gap*, edited by Chuck Collins, Betsy-Leondar Wright, and Holly Sklar, United for a Fair Economy, Boston, MA, 1999; from Lynette Rawlings, *Poverty and Income Trends: 1998*, Center on Budget and Policy Priorities, Washington, DC, 2000, and from other publications of the Center on Budget and Policy Priorities; from L. Jerome Gallagher, Megan Gallagher, Kevin Perese, Susan Schreiber, and Keith Watson, "One Year After Federal Welfare Reform: A Description of State Temporary Assistance for Needy Families (TANF) Decisions as of October 1997," The Urban Institute, Washington, DC, 1998; and from Lawrence Mishel, Jared Bernstein, John Schmitt, and the Economic Policy Institute, *The State of Working America, 1998–99*, Economic Policy Institute, Cornell University, Ithaca, NY, 1999. Used by permission of the publisher, Cornell University Press.

Introduction

I have been involved with welfare most of my life, one way or another. I was a baby when my father died and my mother, working long hours to support her two sons, qualified for what was then called Mother's Pension. That experience with welfare was long behind me when I graduated from social work school and, as some do, I put it out of my mind for years.

Later, however, I worked in a local office of the Maryland State Welfare Department and after a lapse of several years, as deputy assistant secretary of the U.S. Department of Health, Education, and Welfare (now Health and Human Services). Willy nilly—though little is entirely accidental, of course—I was deeply involved in welfare policy. After leaving the government, I taught welfare policy in a university, conducted studies of public assistance practice, and wrote and lectured widely about welfare. So I have known welfare from the inside out, bottom to top, and all around.

When welfare reform was enacted, I did not plan to write a book about it. My views were on the record and writing about it once more, at length, seemed repetitious and boring. Then one day a friend—literate, liberal, socially conscious, and widely informed—leaned across a dinner table and said, "Now tell me, Alvin, why am I against welfare reform?" If Marvin didn't know, it seemed to me that we were truly in trouble; so, perhaps it would be important to make my view of welfare reform available in a more rounded way than op-ed pieces and professional articles permit.

In the end, writing this book proved to be far from boring. The 1996 welfare reform has produced an outpouring of administrative energy and research effort such as has not been seen. All this investment in welfare reform tests the limits of the program's approach to its problems. And a book's requirement to place welfare reform in the context of welfare's troubled history, of the labor market and social attitudes, deepened my understanding of many issues. Finally, the unavoidable requirement to say what should be done now was challenging, not to say intimidating.

The book opens with a brief statement of the general public view, in 1996, of the deficiencies of welfare and the need to reform. Chapter 2 summarizes the reform legislation that was devised to correct these deficiencies. The third chapter reviews the development of welfare or Aid to Dependent Children since 1935, noting that it was devised in a time when mothers were encouraged to stay at home with their children. The program proved not to be adaptable to a society in which mothers are expected to work. In hindsight, one sees other grave problems that were bound to bring the program down.

In Chapter 4, we bring to bear all the evidence that was available by mid-2000 to assess how welfare reform is doing. In the months to come, numerous new reports will appear of studies that have been underway. Details will accumulate and conviction will grow. However, the message that this welfare reform offers can already be read. Much is known about the number of people who went off welfare, about the proportion of those leaving welfare who found work and about their incomes afterwards. In dealing with this material, we begin to see that welfare recipients are not distinctive; they are members of a much larger population of working poor people. For various reasons, some surface in welfare's troubled waters, only to return in time to the status of nonwelfare working poor.

In this chapter, we also examine aspects of welfare reform that are little reported and hardly ever discussed—the large numbers of people turned away arbitrarily ("diverted," administrators say) and "sanctioned" (punished by grant reductions or dropped from assistance entirely because of a perceived failure to meet requirements).

Finally, although there is less evidence about this, we attempt to assess the effect of welfare reform on the way families and children live. Medicaid and food stamps were also addressed in welfare reform legislation; we discuss these programs. We conclude that, although welfare needed to be reformed, the reform that Congress enacted is hurting a good deal more than it is helping.

In order to frame recommendations, in Chapter 5 we turn to issues that underlie broad social policies—first, the expectation that all mothers of young children will work. Welfare reform imposes a formal work requirement on its beneficiaries, but the economy lays the same requirement—effectively, if informally—on mothers in moderate- and middle-income households. We examine this broad social policy.

Chapter 6 brings together material bearing on other broad policies that determine how welfare should be designed or where reform efforts should be directed. Low wages, penurious welfare, and a markedly inferior share of national income for the poorest fifth of the population accompany and, in major degree, account for poverty in the United States. It appears that no one of these "companions" of poverty can be rectified without affecting the others. The chapter sets forth this argument and examines how our goals with respect to wages, poverty, and inequality need to change.

Chapter 7 attempts to forecast the future of welfare programs and of our society at large, if there are no profound changes in policies. It is not a pretty picture.

In Chapter 8, we offer the view, derived in large part from material in earlier chapters, that the nation is unlikely to see the level of change that is required for genuine reform. Nevertheless, we are not excused from offering a program; the remainder of the chapter offers seven guides to devising policies.

The final chapter, outlines major policies that are needed, dealing with wage levels, income maintenance policies (the Earned Income Tax Credit, in particular), policies that particularly concern temporary and part-time workers, and health-care policies. These are by no means all the important policy areas, but these recommendations make clear how other policies ought to develop.

For those who wish it, an appendix provides data on welfare trends over the years, on poverty, and on distribution of income.

The momentum that our now deeply antigovernment, anticommunitarian society has developed takes us in the wrong direction. If we choose to, we can change direction, but it will take a considerable common effort.

August 2000

Acronyms

The following is a list of acronyms found in the book, along with the chapter of first appearance.

AFDC   Originally called Aid to Dependent Children (ADC), the name was changed to Aid to Families with Dependent Children when, in 1961, Congress opened the program to unemployed men in two-parent families. (Chapter 1)

CHIP   Children's Health Insurance Program (Chapter 4)

EITC   Earned Income Tax Credit (Chapter 2)

e.w.a.w.k.i   "end welfare as we know it" (Chapter 2)

FAP   Family Assistance Plan (Appendix B)

HEW   U.S. Department of Health, Education, and Welfare (Chapter 3)

HHS   U.S. Department of Health and Human Services (Chapter 3)

HMO   Health Maintenance Organization (Chapter 7)

HUD	U.S. Department of Housing and Urban Development (Chapter 6)
i.m.	income maintenance (Chapter 4)
INS	U.S. Immigration and Naturalization Service (Chapter 7)
IRS	U.S. Internal Revenue Service (Chapter 8)
MDRC	Manpower Demonstration Research Corporation (Chapter 3)
MFIP	Minnesota Family Investment Program (Chapter 4)
NLRB	National Labor Relations Board (Chapter 9)
NOLEO	Notification of Law Enforcement Officials (Chapter 3)
NWRO	National Welfare Rights Organization (Chapter 3)
SSI	Supplemental Security Income (Chapter 2)
TANF	Temporary Assistance for Needy Families (Chapter 2)
UI	Unemployment Insurance (Chapter 3)
UUCC	Universal Unified Child Credit (Chapter 9)
WWII	World War II (Chapter 3)

Chapter One

The Welfare Narrative

One way we attempt to understand our past is by constructing a narrative. Historians themselves construct a narrative, as becomes evident when succeeding historians reconstruct it. Ernest Renan, a French historian, wrote that "getting history wrong is an essential part of being a nation."[1] And, one might add, it is an essential part of developing broad policy. The narrative that much of our population has accepted about welfare goes like this:

Welfare, that is, Aid to Families with Dependent Children (AFDC, formerly ADC), was created many years ago by President Lyndon Baines Johnson, now remembered for the disastrous war in Vietnam and his war against poverty, or perhaps even longer ago by President Franklin Delano Roosevelt, a towering, if remote, figure.

Undoubtedly, they meant well but failed to take human frailty and greed into account. In particular, they did not face or deal with the inclination of some kinds of people—an underclass, as they have been called—to loll at ease if the government would support them. Why should one work if, without work, a check would arrive regularly anyway? One must acknowledge the trap in which recipients were caught: Anything they earned (or were known to have earned) would reduce their welfare grants, so they really had no incentive to work.

Over the years, one generation of welfare recipients raised another generation who learned to live like this. The government tolerated the spread of a welfare culture that led to wildly rising costs and burdened all taxpayers. Also, many families received far more than they really needed. And, though it may be politically incorrect to say so, the underclass is largely made up of blacks and other minorities.

Because AFDC was chiefly limited to families in which one parent was absent, it created an incentive for men to leave home and, indeed, for unmarried women to have children; after all, the government would support them. Consequently, the numbers of single-parent families and out-of-wedlock children have increased enormously. These people lived on the dole promiscuously, contributing to family breakdown and generally undermining morality.

One cannot overlook the vested interest that bureaucrats and social workers had in perpetuating the program. It provided secure jobs for ten of thousands of them. They were supported and protected by negligent or corrupt politicians, liberals, and others who could not bear to take stern measures.

But why should AFDC mothers be excused from the requirement to earn as much as they can, to support themselves, that all adults face? Moreover, the welfare system undermined children and was bad for adults as well. Children were set an example of what would become for them, in turn, a slothful, immoral, and dependent life.

The program was broken and needed to be discarded. Perhaps it will turn out that the 1996 welfare reform went too far; as difficulties become clear, the country can take corrective measures—within the limits of our resources, of course. We are not a nation that is willing to see children hurt. Still, we don't see all the deprivation that alarmists predicted. Where are they, the people who are suffering?

We revisit this narrative further along, to amplify and correct it.

NOTE

1. Quoted in Eric Alterman, "Untangling Balkan Knots of Myth and Countermyth." *New York Times*, July 31, 1999.

Chapter Two

TANF: The Cure

In August 1996, President Bill Clinton signed an Act of Congress, wiping out AFDC and creating Temporary Assistance for Needy Families (TANF), that is, welfare reform. The sixth "welfare reform" since 1967 (earlier reforms were generally conceded to have achieved very little), TANF was certainly the most sweeping. The president's signature ended four years of discussion, confrontation, and negotiation that were launched when he said, in a 1992 campaign speech, that, if elected, he would "end welfare as we know it" (e.w.a.w.k.i.).[1]

Apparently, he was relying in part on a set of ideas developed by David T. Ellwood, a Harvard professor. Ellwood entered the administration to help convert his ideas into legislation and then left well before welfare reform was enacted, "deeply disappointed"[2] at the course reform was taking. Among other disappointments, he thought a public employment program—which was not proposed—

essential to reform. (Three other high governmental officials re-signed in protest when the president signed the bill.)

The broad popularity with voters of Clinton's promise to "end welfare as we know it" emboldened Republicans to frame a far tougher reform than they had originally had in mind—especially once they assumed control of Congress in 1995. Moreover, they quickly set tough expenditure limits, so the search for budget savings or, at least, the desire to end expenditure increases, added to the determination to reform welfare.

All this was, in a sense, end game. Pressure to devolve programs from the federal government to states, and pressure to reform welfare, in particular, had been building up in the country for years. Under a continuous Reagan-Bush-Clinton policy of waiving federal law to encourage state experimentation, and with President Clinton's e.w.a.w.k.i. signal, thirty-five states were already pursuing a course that foreshadowed the 1996 reform. Not unlike President Clinton's earlier proposals for health-care reform, the change was coming with or without the impetus of federal legislation.

Still, the political situation in Congress, and the president's willingness to sign a bill containing much that he had criticized, put a period (or maybe a semi-colon—much remains to be seen) to a long struggle over the nature of reform.

What, then, did all this controversy lead to? It should be said, in advance, that the reform wiped out an extensive sixty-one-year-old program—AFDC—and made other broad changes. The new program has many parts and is complex.

THE NEW PROGRAM

Old Welfare–New Welfare

Fundamentally, welfare reform eliminated a national safety net for families with children and substituted state-designed programs for categories of families that each state chooses and defines, provided only that beneficiary families include a child.

With AFDC, every eligible family was legally entitled to assistance, but with new welfare, TANF, entitlement to assistance is explicitly ruled out. No family has a legal right to get help, regardless of its circumstances. The effect of this change will be felt dramatically if states experience recession or some other budget crisis, when categories of people whom the state has defined as needy may nevertheless be turned away.

Most requirements for the old-welfare program, such as merit system employment practices, uniform administration throughout a state, and prompt action on applications, have been eliminated. In their place are two basic requirements. First, no family may receive assistance for more than five years in a lifetime. However, states may adopt a lifetime limit shorter than five years, if they wish, and a limited number of exceptions to the time limit are permitted. Second, by 2002, half of all beneficiary families must be working.

The federal government shared heavily in the total cost of old welfare, AFDC, no matter how large the caseload. Under TANF, states receive lump sums of money based on their spending in 1994, without regard to current or anticipated spending. However, they must continue to spend state-matching money at no less than three-quarters of their 1994 expenditure level. As has been indicated, AFDC was extensively regulated by the federal government but TANF administration is "devolved" to the states: they design their own programs.

Nevertheless, a series of specific requirements, focused on the personal behavior of recipients, express TANF's purpose to promote job preparation, work, and marriage. For example, benefits may not be provided to unwed mothers younger than eighteen years old unless they live with an adult relative, or to unwed mothers under eighteen unless they attend school or have a high school diploma. And, parents must perform community service after two months of aid and must work after twenty-four months of aid.

In its most costly year, 1994, AFDC served an average of five million families, more than one in every seven U.S. families with children, at a cost of $14.2 billion in federal funds (1 percent of the federal budget) plus $11.9 billion in state and local funds—$26 billion in all. TANF is providing $16.5 billion a year in federal funds—a $2.3 billion-a-year increase over the federal contribution in the most costly year—through 2002.

Thus, if we ignore inflation, states now receive more than they had been receiving from the federal government, even though their caseloads declined sharply. On top of state revenues that have been increasing anyway, this engenders a measure of satisfaction. On the other hand, federal sharing in AFDC increased automatically with need, but TANF grants are fixed and do not grow larger in any circumstance. This difference will loom large if there is a recession, especially if states divert funds from TANF to other purposes in the meantime. States are permitted to divert up to $40 billion over the course of new welfare's first five years.

RELATED PROGRAM CHANGES

Food Stamps

Food stamps is a voucher program that is more generous in its income limits than AFDC. Families of any sort—unemployed or employed, TANF recipients or not, with or without children, households of one or several people, disabled or not—may use the stamps to purchase food in ordinary retail stores.

These benefits were cut by almost 20 percent, equivalent to reducing the average per-meal allowance of 80 cents to 66 cents. In 1998, nearly seven million families that received food stamps lost an average of $435 in food stamps benefits. Further, unemployed people eighteen to fifty years of age may now receive food stamps for only three months in any thirty-six-month period. It appears that one million jobless people who are willing to work if they can find a job will be denied food stamps because of this provision. All food stamp reductions taken together totaled $28 billion.

In addition, the welfare reform bill reduced allocations for the program that provides meals to children receiving daycare.

Legal Immigrants

Legal immigrants are denied aid that has been provided under Supplemental Security Income (SSI) for the elderly and disabled poor and are denied Medicaid and food stamps. Veterans, refugees, and immigrants granted asylum are excepted from this provision. A subsequent amendment to the law restored these benefits for legal immigrants who were already being assisted when the president signed the new-welfare law, but not for new applicants.

SSI for Disabled Children

Disabling conditions that qualify children for SSI were substantially narrowed. For example, children suffering from multiple disabilities no one of which meets the criteria established for the bill are no longer eligible for assistance, although they may have been before. Some 315,000 low-income children who would have qualified under old-welfare law will be denied SSI by 2002, according to estimates of the Congressional Budget Office.

Medicaid

Families receiving AFDC were automatically entitled to Medicaid. With Congress concerned that people would resist leaving AFDC for TANF or for work if it would mean losing Medicaid, the law provides that they would be entitled to Medicaid for one year more after leaving the program. We return to this and to the impact of other TANF provisions in Chapter 4.

THE EARNED INCOME TAX CREDIT

On a separate track from AFDC or TANF, the Earned Income Tax Credit (EITC) has developed into a substantial cash income maintenance program. Nearly twenty million families and individuals filing tax returns in 1999 claimed this benefit. Modest at its start in 1975, the EITC has been expanded over the years so that, in 1999, a family with two or more children might receive as much as $3,816.

Designed to encourage work, the benefit is very small at the lowest earning levels, increases gradually to provide the maximum benefit for a person earning about $12,000 a year, declines gradually as earnings increase, and phases out entirely at earnings of $30,580. Benefits for a family with one child are smaller and are very modest indeed for a worker with no children. A person at home with children and not working is not entitled to benefits.

The EITC is administered by the Internal Revenue Service (IRS) as part of the income tax system; the tax return is the application for benefits. It is a credit against any tax due; any remainder is paid out as a refund. The EITC pre-dates and is not a provision of TANF. It is described here to help in clarifying material that follows.

NOTES

1. Jason DeParle, "Success, and Frustration, as Welfare Rules Change." *New York Times*, December 30, 1997. P. 1.

2. David T. Ellwood, "Welfare Reform As I Knew It." *The American Prospect*, May–June 1996, no. 26, p. 28.

Chapter Three

Six Decades of Welfare

We revisit the welfare narrative to provide a fuller sense of the source of its ambiguities and misperceptions and to glean such lessons as may be taken from experience.

The old-welfare program was enacted in 1935, during the Great Depression, as it was called. ADC was part of a package of legislation proposed by President Franklin Delano Roosevelt that included social security and unemployment insurance (UI). Social security and UI would "insure" against the financial problems of most people, but there had to be a program for those who would remain unprotected. This program, derived from earlier models called Mother's Pensions, was ADC.

ADC was highly selective at first; in particular, staffs tended to deny benefits to blacks and unmarried mothers. The U.S. Children's Bureau and powerful child advocates argued that ADC should be limited to "nice" families, as Mother's Pensions had been. They feared that helping too many families that were "not nice" would lead to public opprobrium and sink the program for everyone. As time passed, these advocates for a "nice" program undoubtedly concluded that events had proved them right.

Even so, from the beginning, federal policy statements emphasized that the program was not to be selective. Rather, homes that were substandard should be helped to improve and, if that was not possible, children were to be removed and placed in foster homes. For years, states skirted these pronouncements; by 1960, twenty-three states excluded families that did not provide "suitable homes." In 1961, however, after Louisiana had summarily terminated assistance to more than 6,000 families because they were considered unsuitable, the U.S. Department of Health, Education, and Welfare (HEW) ruled that states that operated under such draconian policies would lose federal funding. To such a threat states paid attention.

With the states under pressure, more blacks and single mothers received assistance. The proportion of blacks in the caseloads rose from one in seven, nationally, to a high of just under half in 1973. Then it slowly declined to about a third in 1995; whites constituted about the same proportion and white and nonwhite Hispanics accounted for most of the remainder.

So AFDC was never a majority-black program, and substantial numbers of white—at times, constituting a majority—were always beneficiaries. Unmarried mothers went from hardly any in the early years to one-third of the caseload in 1973 and more than half by 1986.

Only a small part of the program's opening up can be attributed to more hospitable state administration. The more significant message is that AFDC, planned for a society that seems to us today to have been puritanical and deeply tainted with racism, was swamped by rapid social change. The following changes are a roll call of the restructuring of post-World War II America.

1. The civil rights movement swept the country in the 1960s and discriminatory practices that had seemed natural came to be rejected, at least in public discourse. Drawing power from this movement and with the government as a sometimes tacit but often

outspoken ally, the National Welfare Rights Organization (NWRO) was successful, to a degree, in liberalizing policy and enforcing observance of welfare regulations.

It should be emphasized that the civil rights movement and the NWRO were successful only in part and only for a while. As Martin Gilens makes clear in a subtly reasoned book called *Why Americans Hate Welfare* (1999), racial stereotypes have animated welfare policy and still do today. Indeed, the relative stinginess of a state's benefit levels can be predicted by the percentage of blacks in its caseload.

2. In the 1930s, women were actively discouraged from working outside their homes: AFDC was *designed* to keep mothers at home. World War II drew women into employment in large numbers; after 1960, their numbers increased steadily. By the 1990s, 60 percent of mothers with preschool children were working. It was in this climate that the concept of incentive to work hit home as a problem.

That is, welfare levels did not nearly support a decent living arrangement. At the same time, AFDC mothers were required to report earnings so they could be deducted from their monthly payments. Thus, the kind of low-paid work they could find did not improve their income at all. The families were trapped with paupers' incomes. Yet, with so many other women at work, the question of why welfare recipients should be privileged not to work was asked again and again.

Seeking a way out, in 1967 Congress enacted a "30 & 1/3 rule": AFDC mothers would have their first $30 of wages and one-third of the remainder deducted in fixing their monthly payment. Thus, earnings would add modestly—very modestly—to their welfare income and should provide them with incentive to work. When this provision appeared to have little effect, succeeding Congresses fine-tuned it but never managed to alter the public perception of "the welfare trap."

3. Propelled by the drive of women for a new social role, the American family has changed in ways that greatly altered and expanded AFDC's clientele. The new social role of women included a new role in the workforce, a lengthening life span for men and

women, and increasingly tolerant attitudes about sexual relations—in practice, if not always rhetorically.

In the 1930s, for example, there were as many widows heading
families as mothers who were divorced or separated and comparatively few mothers who had never been married. Today there are
fewer widows with young children and many more mothers who
have divorced or separated; over a third of single mothers have
never married at all. Thus, even as the administration of AFDC
gradually became more open to such mothers, many more were
applying. Those accepted would be increasingly "not nice." The
problem was accentuated by the expansion of social security to
cover widows in 1939; widows would no longer be applying for
AFDC.

In this connection, we note that in the 1960s, chemical drugs replaced alcohol as the prevalent addictive agent. Some, like crack
cocaine which came on the scene in the 1980s, were virulent in their
effect on families and on family members' capacity to earn a living.

4. The Great Depression ended with the Second World War,
which was followed in turn by the "affluent fifties." Despite reces-
sions between 1958 and 1960, in the 1970s, and again in the 1980s,
the overall trend was to dramatic increases in wealth and income.
The proportion of all Americans who were poor declined from 22
percent in 1959 to 13 percent in 1977, but child poverty remains
high at about 20 percent.[1]

Possibly more significant is that the number of poor children in
deep poverty[2] rose steadily, from 30 percent in 1975 to almost 40 percent in 1997. That is, the situation of poor children is growing even
more desperate. This, too, would create a larger pool of candidates
for AFDC.

5. Between 1940 and 1957, one million people a year migrated
from farms. As farming industrialized, Mississippi, a state that
maintained a population of about 2.2 million overall throughout
this period, lost more than 900,000 blacks. When these migrants
moved north and west looking for work in factories (and the evidence is that the impetus to move was usually the prospect of
work), and when some lost jobs they had found, many applied for

welfare. As programs almost anywhere were more liberal than in Mississippi, they qualified more readily and represented a net addition to the national welfare caseload and its proportion of blacks.

Thus, one may understand why all these developments, taken together, inflated the number of individuals in recipient families—from 500,000 in 1936, to three million in 1960, to fourteen million in 1995. It was consequential but curious that Congress steadily liberalized eligibility for AFDC, even as it criticized its rising cost. The cost (in 1996 dollars) rose from $265 million in 1936, to $6 billion in 1960, to $26 billion in 1995. (The federal share of these sums in 1995, a little more than half, was still only 1 percent of the federal budget.) These costs and the poor fit of AFDC to the changing society in which it was embedded provoked sporadic outbursts of adverse public reaction and attempts at correction and reform.

REACTION AND REFORM

In the very beginning, AFDC enjoyed a moratorium on criticism, but then public reaction became steadily more critical and resentful. Early on, there were some complaints about immorality, but little complaint about mothers not working; that was the norm, after all. And during WW II, the public was occupied with larger matters than AFDC.

After the war, however, complaints tended to reflect inflammatory social issues as they arose. After costs soared in the late 1940s and 1950s, bitter charges of fraud and cheating were leveled. As juvenile delinquency rates rose, the U.S. Senate held hearings on AFDC and instructed HEW to study its connection with delinquency. Similarly, it required a study of the connection between AFDC and unmarried parenthood. In general, *causal* connections were not found. AFDC, juvenile delinquency, and unmarried parenthood are all associated with poverty, however.

In response to criticism, states made it a condition of eligibility that the family's home must provide a "suitable" environment for children, and many states and localities launched investigations of cheating and fraud. We noted earlier that in 1961 HEW barred suitable home requirements; states then turned to a rule about "the man in the house," ending assistance if a man was present, and to other euphemisms for "suitable home." To look into these matters, Maine set up the nation's first special investigation unit, operating separately from social work staff.

This separation reflected distrust of social workers and bureaucrats, who were to join their clients among the accused—accused of being sentimentally overgenerous and of being careless with government money. Other states followed Maine; in time, across the country, investigators surveilled homes of recipients and conducted "midnight raids" in the hope of surprising a man in the house. Ultimately, courts found these raids to be unconstitutional, warrantless invasions.

In 1961, all the issues came together in Newburgh, New York, a town that became a symbol of national discontent. Newburgh was losing white, middle-class residents; in their place, migratory workers were settling down. Rising costs for welfare seemed unbearable. Newburgh packaged policies old and new, many of doubtful legality that were quietly being practiced elsewhere, in a proposed plan.

For example, aid would be in the form of vouchers for food, clothing, or housing, not as cash that might be used for liquor or carousing. Or, applicants who were "new to the city" would be limited to one or two weeks of aid. The term was an early appearance of requirements that AFDC applicants establish that they are legal residents of the state in which they seek aid. These were eventually ruled unconstitutional, only to turn up later in other guises. Or, aid was to be denied to unmarried mothers who had another child after receiving assistance. Or, recipients would be required to accept work assignments—by no means a new idea, but new for AFDC.

The New York Social Welfare Board investigated, found the Newburgh plan to be contrary to the Social Security Act, and forbade implementation. The town's city manager, Joseph Mitchell, had meanwhile gathered wide and passionate support for the plan; he hesitated, but had to comply. Nevertheless, the proposed solutions gained national attention, including support from Senator Barry Goldwater, then in the early states of seeking the Republican Party nomination for the presidency.

One cannot review this outline without appreciating the depth of anger about AFDC since WW II. Nor should it be thought that these reactions were unique to AFDC or to this period. One of many who have made the point over the years, Rutgers University Law School Professor Philip Harvey wrote in 1999 that public responses to people without jobs in late medieval England and in modern America, when they seek means-tested aid, are remarkably similar. "Jobless individuals were viewed as persons of suspect moral character who chose to live lives of idleness rather than accept presumptively available employment."[3]

CONGRESS AND REFORM

In improving AFDC in the 1950s and 1960, as ever, Congress was more inclined to fiddle than to compose. The first of a series of narrowly focused, carelessly thought-through federal changes was the so-called NOLEO provision ("Notification of Law Enforcement Officials" when a parent failed to provide financial support for a child). Congress imagined that prosecutors would indict errant fathers and secure support, but prosecutors, occupied with matters that struck them as more important, ignored the law.

In succeeding years, Congress fortified NOLEO with more explicit instructions to states about exacting parental support, with a federal Family Locator Service that would help to find fathers and with funding tied to carrying out these functions. However, it was only when DNA testing became available to prove parenthood that newer and stronger provisions, in the 1988 Family Support Act, were able to invigorate family support activity.

In reaction to criticism about breaking up families, 1961 legislation authorized states to open AFDC to unemployed men in two-parent families. Out of concern about potential costs, however, Congress defined this program so narrowly—chiefly by limiting the number of hours that unemployed recipients could be working—that by 1996 it accounted for less than 10 percent of total benefits. Nor did the provision appear demonstrably to have reduced separations or divorce.

Ruling on the fracas about suitable homes when Louisiana terminated asseptance to 6,000 families, HEW had required states to provide AFDC and, if necessary, to assist families to improve their homes. Where this could not be successful, children were to be removed to foster care. As states turned out to have difficulty in paying for foster care, in 1961 Congress undertook to pay for such provision.

PRECURSORS TO THE 1996 WELFARE REFORM

Tough Love

Of broader consequence to welfare families than any of the measures named just above, was a plan pursued state by state and never enacted by Congress. AFDC payment levels had been rising very slowly from the parsimonious levels—about $13 a month per child in 1940—at which they began. In the early 1970s, however, states turned them downward and then they declined year by year. See Appendix A, Table A-5.

In 1970, the average monthly AFDC check per family was $734 (in 1996 dollars), but in recent years never more than $389, which was slightly more than half the 1970 payment level. This was a far cry from the official government poverty level. To be sure, AFDC was usually supplemented by food stamps. In a 1997 book based on a painstaking and practical study of AFDC families, Kathryn Edin and Laura Lein (1997) estimated that AFDC and food stamps, taken together, covered only 60 percent of mothers' expenses.

It should be illuminating to think of this quarter century of declining payment levels as an experiment that went before the 1996 welfare reform. Steadily declining levels shared a tacit assumption with the 1996 reform, that is, that want would drive women to work. Presumably, some were driven to work, but caseloads and costs rose sharply during this period and, in general, the "experiment" failed. Among the reasons that the women did not go to work—chiefly that there were not decent jobs for them—was that their families' need would not have been moderated. According to Edin and Lein (1997), income from work would have covered only 63 percent of their expenses.

Social Services

As Congress became concerned about dependency, delinquency, and illegitimacy, it was advised that social services, that is, such services as counseling, psychiatric treatment when necessary, daycare for children, and homemaker service when someone in the home required care, would strengthen families and would permit or encourage AFDC mothers to work. The advice was warmly offered and persuasive.

In 1956, therefore, Congress amended AFDC law to emphasize social services. When states did not seem to respond to legislative encouragement, in 1962 Congress added cash subsidies for social services. However, this did not produce visible results in terms of work or stronger families, either. To be sure, it is doubtful whether services of good quality were ever widely delivered.

Congressional interest in welfare-to-work programs hardened in 1967. Frustrated with failure to get improvement without stern measures, the House Ways and Means Committee designed the first Work Incentive Program (dubbed WIN to avoid having it known as WIP). WIN required states to assure that "appropriate" relatives of an AFDC child would go to work. Together with the U.S. Department of Labor, states would provide necessary counseling, training, and childcare.

However, Congress did not appropriate the sums of money that were necessary—a chronic failing; nor did states provide required matching for the federal money that was available—also a chronic failing. And there were few jobs for people with the education and experience that AFDC parents could muster. A review in 1991 by the Manpower Demonstration Research Corporation (MDRC) called *From Welfare to Work* observes that, in the outcome, "the program was judged inadequate for not delivering on the promise of change."[4]

Attempts were made to tighten WIN and improve the delivery of services. Still, a history of welfare by Blanche Coll (1995) records that WIN "failed to score significantly . . . to substitute workfare for welfare, to cut the AFDC rolls."[5]

The accretion of tough-love measures and social services was interrupted in August 1969 by President Richard Nixon's proposal of a sweeping income guarantee (see Appendix B) for families with children. There was much support from liberals, who saw this as "a foot in the door," a commitment to a guaranteed income that might eventually be improved to a reasonable level; from conservatives, who saw an opportunity to wipe out the welfare system and the social workers and bureaucrats who went with it; and from many who simply felt that welfare had to be replaced somehow.

In the end, however, the proposal was defeated in Congress in 1972. The politics had been byzantine and evidently the president had quietly withdrawn his support for the bill. Moreover, as prominent economist Alice Rivlin later said about proposals like the president's, "We were technically naïve. . . . We simply did not understand how complicated practical problems were."[6] The dense cloud of national controversy that surrounded the proposal lasted for several years, accompanied by mounting denunciations of welfare and welfare recipients and demands for reform.

Congress returned to social services with the Family Support Act of 1988—carefully named to dramatize the hype surrounding its enactment. Even more firmly than earlier legislation, the law required clients to engage in training or work and emphasized collection of child support from fathers and the provision of child care and other social services. As with earlier legislation, it was never fully funded and failed to deliver on its promises.

Between broad and deep citizen anger about welfare, general blindness to, if not tolerance of, the pauperization of the welfare population, and repeated failure of *weak* tough-love/social service measures, the ground had been prepared for the 1996 welfare reform described in Chapter 2.

ACCUSATIONS AND EVIDENCE

Despite countless studies with contrary findings over the years, many baseless charges about AFDC survive, because they have become conventional wisdom and because conservative pundits who are, at best, careless continue to broadcast them. The list that follows offers relevant data and relies especially on the *1998 Green Book* of the Ways and Means Committee of the U.S. House of Representatives (1999).

- *Who Received AFDC?* Children, typically under six years of age, and their mothers, usually over twenty-five years of age. She was unemployed and divorced or separated. The child's father did not live with them and did not receive AFDC. The average family had three members—a mother and two children.

- *How Many Teenagers Were on Welfare?* One out of fifteen AFDC mothers was in her teens.

- *What About Unmarried Mothers at Any Age?* In 1969, about one in four AFDC children had unmarried parents; by 1995, more than one-half.

Comment: the sharp increase in the number of unmarried AFDC mothers from 1969 to 1995 tracks with general population change. The rate of marriage in the total population fell by 43 percent between 1960 and 1997, so unmarried women now account for one-third of all births in the United States. This statistic underscores a point that almost everyone knows: marriage, failure to marry, and out-of-wedlock births are products of social forces that affect all families, AFDC families among them.

- *Did Welfare Encourage Larger Families?* With an average payment of an additional $80 a month for adding another child to the family in the 1990s, few women would have thought it financially profitable to become pregnant. In fact, between 1960 and 1995, the size of the average AFDC family *declined* from 3.8 to 2.8. The typical number of children in an AFDC family fell from three to two.

Comment: during the 1960s, the birth control pill and Medicaid-financed abortion became available to poor people for the first time. It seems eminently plausible that, with abortion and convenient contraception available to them, AFDC mothers set out to have more nearly the number of children that they wanted—two rather than the three that women in welfare once had.

- *Was Welfare a Way of Life?* Well over half of all episodes on welfare ended within their first year. Still, most recipients returned to the program within two years, many to exit again in a year or two. (Major factors in leaving welfare were work and support from the child's father; major reasons for returning were the birth of another child and losing a job or outside support.) Adding all episodes on welfare, two-thirds of families received AFDC for a cumulative total of five years or less. Looking at the question about a way of life another way, almost three out of four recipients received as much as half their income from AFDC and food stamps, taken together, for less than two years, according to a year 2000 report by the U.S. Department of Health and Human Services (HHS).[7] That is, half their income or more was from work or child support. In sum, it would not be a close description to say that *welfare* was a way of life for welfare families, in general.

  Comment: one year after leaving welfare, half of the families were poor; five years afterward, 40 percent of the families were poor. A statement closer to reality would be to say that very low income imposes a way of life; when work and support proved entirely inadequate, mothers regarded welfare as one more potential resource.

- *Does One Generation on Welfare Raise Another?* The large majority of children in welfare families did *not* grow up to depend on welfare. However, it is a fact that welfare children were statistically more likely to wind up on AFDC than the average of all other children. Was this because some family dynamic or model influenced a girl or, on the other hand, because she shared with her family a poor education, no resources, and no influence at school or at work? Research does not add up to a convincing conclusion, one way or the other.

- *Did Welfare Families Live on the Fat of the Land?* Some fat of the land! See "Tough Love" above.
- *Where Are They, the People Who Are Suffering?* They are everywhere around us, just as the poor were everywhere around us when, in *The Other America* (1964), Michael Harrington called our attention to the "invisible poor." We return to this in more detail further along.

WHAT MIGHT ONE LEARN?

The history of AFDC is characterized by sustained public hostility and racism, reflected in the administration of AFDC and only incompletely suppressed from time to time by the federal government. Public resentment seemed to rise and fall in relation to larger events—the Second World War, family trends, anxiety about the federal budget, the civil rights movement and, no doubt, immigration, recession, and unemployment levels. Yet, except at the program's very beginning, there was always citizen anger and a sense of mounting frustration.

Viewing AFDC over sixty years or so, it may seem a miracle that it survived so long—never mind "survived," was, in various ways, steadily liberalized[8] even as attempts were being made to cut it back. Any number of people who managed or whose parents managed a little more easily because of AFDC have reason to feel grateful that it did. One reason that the program survived may be that somehow, until the 1990s, no one even dreamed of wiping it out.

Why did so many efforts at correction and reform fail? Like success, every failure has a thousand fathers: because Congress consistently failed fully to fund reforms that legislation authorized; because many states failed to provide matching money even for the federal funds that were available; in the case of reforms focused on work, because jobs were not available at even poverty-level wages at the educational or skill level of AFDC parents.

Many of the support services were poorly conceived and poorly organized. Just as states skirted the edges of federal regulations, so they did not assure daycare of decent quality for young children whose mothers were told to be somewhere else, and did not provide the skilled counseling that social service funding intended. The federal-oversight/state-administered structure of AFDC requires a largely shared view of what is intended and it was not there from the beginning.

AFDC was not designed for a society in which mothers want to work and, whether they want to or not, must work. Reforms tinkered with, but did not resolve, the incentive issue. Perhaps as much as anything else, reforms failed because AFDC was not intended to be a large program; it was intended to deal with minor gaps in broad coverage. There were to be insurance-like protections (social security, unemployment insurance) for the income of the husband or widow. In contemporary circumstances, many mothers and children are not protected by these programs and, although there are working models in other countries, we have never settled on an acceptable insurance-like program for our mothers and children.

Designed in a time when many people were in trouble, AFDC was created by a care-for-your-neighbor, comparatively generous society and, three generations removed from the Great Depression of the 1930s, we are today, at least as we express ourselves through our government, an everyone-for-yourself, sink-or-swim society.

One may learn from the record that a program must have or be able to achieve a level of common public acceptance to work well for a long time. It must be administered by units that accept its basic objectives. Its operations must achieve some threshold of funding adequacy. It cannot set objectives that everything around it frustrates, as if a hospital thought itself principally responsible for maintaining a healthy population, or a relief program thought itself principally responsible for maintaining a moral society or providing a healthy job market at decent wages.

AFDC was dysfunctional and the citizenry was not in sympathy with it. It required replacement, but surely not by TANF. In the chapters that follow, we examine the difficulties that TANF poses and major policy issues that one must resolve in order to arrive at alternate ways to proceed.

NOTES

1. The Census Bureau is seriously considering a revision of the government's definition of poverty, which has basically been unaltered since 1965. Family needs and patterns have changed considerably, affecting the basis for the definition. Also, noncash income such as food stamps is not reflected in the income that is counted.

Almost any revised definition that has been proposed would increase the proportion of Americans counted as poor; and the proportion of children counted as poor would substantially exceed 20 percent.

2. Currently, deep poverty means that one's family income is less than 50 percent of the government poverty level, that is, is less than $7,500 a year for a family of three.

3. Philip Harvey, "Joblessness and the Law Before the New Deal." *Georgetown Journal on Poverty Law & Policy*, v. VI, no. 1, Winter 1999, p. 41.

4. Judith M. Gueron and Edward Pauly with Cameron M. Lougy, *From Welfare to Work*. Manpower Demonstration Research Corporation: New York and San Francisco, 1991. P. 8.

5. Blanche D. Coll, *Safety Net: Welfare and Social Security, 1929–1979*, New Brunswick, NJ: Rutgers University Press, 1995. P. 249.

6. Alice M. Rivlin, Discussion of papers by James Tobin and Robert J. Lampman, at the Annual Meeting of the American Statistical Association. New York, December 27–30, 1973. *Proceedings*. American Statistical Association: Washington, D.C., 1974.

7. *Indicators of Welfare Dependence*, Annual Report to Congress, March 2000. U.S. Department of Health and Human Services. Table SUM3.

8. In liberalizing AFDC payment levels, Congress was no doubt influenced by generally rising living standards in the 1960s.

Chapter Four

The Cure That Does Not Cure

Never very comfortable, welfare clients are even worse off today than they have been in many years. By 1998, about a third of them were working, a goal specified in the 1996 reform legislation, and caseloads had dropped by almost half from their 1994 peak. Public attention focused on this kind of outcome, creating an impression that reform was succeeding.

On the other hand, in the prosperous time after the 1996 legislation, the average income of all single parents and of welfare clients in particular declined. After welfare reform, the poorest 20 percent of single-parent families, typically families who had left welfare, *lost* an average of $577 a year. A national study of "welfare leavers" in 1997, reported by Pamela Loprest for the Urban Institute (1999), found that one-third of them reported having to cut meal sizes or skip meals; almost 40 percent had problems with paying rent, mortgage or utility bills.[1] Other problems also became apparent; we shall come to these.

The first important effect of welfare reform that we record is a change in the culture of the welfare departments that was, in effect, mandated by the welfare reform legislation. Taking note of this may help in making sense of what followed.

THE CULTURE OF WELFARE DEPARTMENTS

Over the years, there has been much discussion about the culture of welfare recipients. In conventional wisdom, they were not ambitious, not strivers, and not particularly guarded about their morals—sexual or otherwise. However, the culture of those with whom the recipients dealt, the welfare *workers*, was not much attended to. In the 1960s, the workers' attitude to recipients shifted from friendly, paternalistic, or neutral to generally hostile.

Before that, the philosophy of ADC had been that its clients were deeply troubled and needed help and guidance—that is, social work guidance. After 1960, the philosophy was that decisions to award cash assistance (or not) should focus strictly on meeting legal qualifications. Clerical employees, who could do this more efficiently, replaced social workers. The deepest effect of this change lay not so much in a loss of professionalism—there had not been much professionalism anyway—but in the shift from experienced income maintenance (i.m.) workers who knew the clients to inexperienced workers. The new i.m. workers were often uncertain about their roles and sometimes frightened by the militant clients of the 1960s. Staff members became reluctant to visit clients in their homes, a long-standing practice, and security guards began to appear in welfare offices. The cultures of the i.m. workers and of their clients were now plainly adversarial.

Buffeted by sustained public criticism, declining morale, greatly increased micromanagement by legislatures, and various other unfortunate developments, welfare administration deteriorated. A phenomenon developed that was called "churning": People were cut off only to reapply within a month or two and demonstrate eligibility. Presumably, they had been eligible all the time but someone—the recipient or the worker—had made an error. Although churning became widespread, there was no serious attempt at correction right up to 1996. This was an indication of the system's problem, a compound of baroque bureaucracy and worker indifference or outright hostility to clients.

However, the 1996 welfare reform, Temporary Assistance for Needy Families (TANF), was premised on offering vigorous help to clients to gain skills and supports that they would need to hold jobs rather than simply to collect assistance. Many experts were quietly dubious that welfare workers would be able to take a supportive (if not sympathetic) role; so experts were surprised by what appeared to them to be a rapid changeover to the new approach.

Official assertions about the operations of the welfare system have been characteristically at odds with real-life practice. Before 1960, welfare was said to be humanistic and oriented to social services, but agencies were really oriented to cash assistance and personal help was scant. Following 1960, the system was said to be oriented to legal rights, but all the while churning was increasing and studies showed that as many as 50 percent of those who were eligible were turned away. Rhetoric and reality were similarly at odds after welfare reform in 1996. A radical difference in the way welfare departments described their work and a genuine attempt to offer this changed approach in a few localities led experts to believe that they had underestimated the adaptability of the departments. Alas, for the acuity of these experts.

All the talk about reform highlighted encouragement to work, offers of training, and the investment of workers (now called caseworkers) in shoring up the self-esteem of their clients. Caught between ingrained institutional hostility and these promises of helpfulness, workers fused the two into a didactic, possibly even a hectoring, approach to clients: "You have to dress neatly. You have to get there on time. You are as good as you want to be. You *can* do this!" And so forth. But there has not been much of the listening that counseling entails and not much responsiveness.

Readers of *The New York Times* may remember a long article by Jason DeParle in 1999, setting forth the heroic efforts, at extraordinary personal sacrifice, of a Milwaukee caseworker, Michael

Steinborn, to help his clients. However, Steinborn's efforts were literally unique. Wisconsin and other states were more interested in reducing their caseloads than in helping recipients; and their caseworkers got the message.

DeParle devoted all of 1999 to watching the welfare reform effort in Wisconsin, a poster state of national welfare reform. By the end of the year, he was getting discouraged; the closing article in his series was headlined "Bold Effort Leaves Much Unchanged for the Poor." In this article, DeParle writes: "Conceptually, it is an impressive effort to demand work and support. Operationally, it has often been a mess, a tangle of unresponsive bureaucracies, uninspired casework and so much initial chaos and confusion that many needy families still express contempt at the [program]."[2]

Across the country, welfare worker negativism was more painfully reflected in turning way applications for assistance. Hearing a class action lawsuit, Judge William Pauley III of Federal District Court in New York complained about "a culture of improper deterrence at job centers"[3] that drove the needy away. A practice developed of "testing the job market" before providing cash aid or counseling. That is, applicants were told to try to find work and return after several weeks if they could not. It was not as if none of them had been looking for work, and some were desperate.

By 1999, thirty-one states had developed "diversion" programs. Along with mandatory job searches, these included lump sum payments in lieu of TANF and instruction to seek help from family, friends, and private charities. With broad discretion, diversion programs offered caseworkers wide range for exercising personal judgment, not to say personal bias. Rejections at intake, tacit or outright, were just as responsible for declining caseloads as were the graduations from the rolls of those who had received welfare.

This is all to say that, as a practical matter, most welfare workers and most departments were more interested in denying or terminating assistance than in counseling or supporting clients. The reform had grown out of deep public anger at welfare clients; moreover, the federal government was now requiring steep reductions in caseloads. Why would welfare workers, who had been schooled to hostility over the years, modify a culture perfectly suited to their feelings and to the government's real purpose?

WELFARE REFORM: THE JOB MARKET

The evolution of employment patterns in the 1990s has been widely discussed and the term "dual labor market," which has not been heard for some years, is staging a reappearance. Lower-tier work—dead-end work, as it was once called—is performed by the poorly trained and poorly educated. Offering poor pay, scant fringe benefits, and little opportunity for advancement, it is walled off from higher-tier work.

Primarily because of technological change and transfers of job opportunities to overseas employers, the number of domestic industrial jobs—lower paid than in 1973 but still *relatively* high—is declining. In their place, we have service-sector employment—fast food, hotels, the entertainment industry, retail sales—which is much more poorly paid. At $5.15, an hour and, indeed, at $6.15 an hour—proposed but not enacted by the end of 2000, the minimum wage has failed to keep pace with the cost of living, not to mention with increasing productivity and affluence.

The rift that was always visible between the lower and upper tiers of the labor market has widened into a continental divide. As $7.00 an hour is required for one person working full-time all year to reach the poverty level for a three-person family (or $8.50 an hour for a four-person family), the lower tier includes the so-called working poor. The Earned Income Tax Credit (see Chapter 2) adds to income from work, of course.

Welfare recipients tend to qualify only for work in the lower tier. The education of recipients does not prepare or qualify them for higher-end work. (We do not even speak of work related to computers or in the professions.) Studies show that two out of five have not attended high school and the average recipient reads at the sixth-grade level. In-depth studies in Kansas, Washington, and Utah found that one-fifth to one-third or more of current recipients have learning disabilities. An irony of welfare reform is that federal work requirements forced recipients who were attending college—20,000 in New York City alone—to drop out.

Recipients have a variety of other handicaps with respect to employment. Many do not have recent work experience. All have a child or children, most of them needing care during the day that costs more than a fifth of the parent's income, on the average—if daycare is available at all. Most recipients are single parents, which means that a sick child presents a tough problem about getting to work on time or at all.

Many recipients live in ghetto areas of our cities, with poor public transportation to suburban areas where many job openings are. For example, a study at Case Western Reserve University in Cleveland revealed that more than half of the job openings in the region could not be reached in less than 80 minutes.[4] Almost half of the recipients have health problems. An Urban Institute study by Sheila Zedlewski in 1999 calculated that more than four out of ten recipients reported at least two "significant obstacles to work."[5]

With welfare reform, caseloads have been markedly reduced and goals specified in the legislation about the proportion of TANF recipients who must be working generally have been met. However, state reports of such proportions may be impeachable because states are able to manipulate their statistics and have a financial stake in reporting that they meet federal goals. Furthermore, 15 percent of recipients—half of those now reported working—were working *before* welfare reform. Still, the percentage reported to be working after welfare reform doubled.

It appears that those recipients who were working had substantial earnings but—with exceptions—failed to increase their total income (from work and welfare together) over the income they had had from welfare alone. Either way, they usually had less income than the poverty level. Exceptions, observed in a Manpower Demonstration Research Corporation (MDRC) study in Florida, were people who had entered the project with recent work experience and at least a high school degree. These are a minority of recipients and they are the most likely to have found their way out of welfare on their own, as many AFDC recipients regularly did. Whether the children in any of these work-and-welfare families flourished or languished, few studies reveal.

How recipients fare *after* they leave welfare completely may be more significant than their experience while still receiving welfare. It appears that between half and three-quarters of parents are employed shortly after leaving the rolls. They don't earn much—typically less than $8 an hour and often less than $6 an hour. As their work is often temporary (an average of seven or eight months) and sporadic, their annual income is markedly less than the hourly rate suggests. And many do not receive paid vacation or sick leave benefits.

The Pamela Loprest study referred to earlier tells the story: The majority of those who leave welfare do, indeed, fit into the labor market—at "the low end of the labor market."[6] More than a quarter of them work mostly at night; over half struggle with arranging child care. Roughly a third return to welfare within a few months. One in five is not working and does not have any other discernible source of income. A third of those who leave welfare skip meals or cut the size of meals and they have trouble with mortgage or utility payments or paying the rent. They face unremitting financial pressure.

No Shame in My Game, a 1999 book by Katherine S. Newman that is based on interviews with 300 New Yorkers over two years, provides more sense of immediacy about the anxious and chaotic lives that the working poor lead: "one paycheck away from what is left of welfare, one sick child away from getting fired, one missed rent payment short of eviction. They want nothing more than additional work hours to increase their earning . . . but they can easily be reduced to indigence."[7] Most of what has been reported in this chapter was in a period when unemployment rates were as low as they had ever been and the economy was flying high.

Minnesota

Minnesota's Family Investment Program (MFIP) was uniquely generous in design compared with the other states. Because of its differences and because it has received wide attention, it deserves some discussion of its own. The following material is drawn largely from reports in 2000 of an extensive, careful, three-year evaluation by the Manpower Demonstration Research Corporation (MDRC).[8]

Single parents who had received welfare for more than two years and who took a job were allowed to keep more of their welfare benefits. For example, a mother who worked part-time would receive $599 a month under MFIP compared to $362 under the old program. They were now required to work or participate in activities that would lead to work. Those who had received welfare for less than two years benefited from the same incentive arrangements but were not required to work.

Both groups benefited from greatly simplified rules and social services were enriched, particularly for the long-term recipients.

MFIP produced strikingly positive results for long-term single-parent recipients. After twenty-seven months, their employment rates were higher than for the comparison group; they registered a 15 percent increase in family income. Effects for recent applicants were also positive, but much smaller. Both long-term and short-term single-parent MFIP participants were *more* likely to continue on welfare than AFDC comparison groups. This was predictable, as modestly higher incomes did not disqualify MFIP participants.

As for two-parent families in MFIP, at least one of the two parents worked at the same rate as in AFDC two-parent comparison groups, but the couples earned less, in total, because one partner or the other had cut back on work hours or left a job. This finding is reminiscent of experiments conducted in the 1970s in connection with "guaranteed income" proposals (see Appendix B). With a modest income "guaranteed," some women reduced work hours to stay at home with children and some men left work or reduced work hours to search for better jobs.

As with improvements in income and employment, long-term (two years or more) single-parent families reported improvements in family functioning. Children were getting better grades in school, they had fewer behavioral problems, and so forth. Much was made in the media of the finding that, after three years, more women in the MFIP group than in the AFDC comparison group were married—10.6 percent compared to 7 percent. It is an interesting finding, interesting to speculate about, but one should not get carried away. Eighty-nine percent and 93 percent, respectively, of the two groups were still not married. Two-parent families also showed substantial increases in marital stability.

As with much research, after the fact the findings seem obvious: If you require work, and there are jobs (Minnesota's unemployment rate dropped to 2.5 percent in 1998), and there are ways to have children cared for *and you make it really worthwhile*, people will increase work or go to work. Even so, some MFIP groups did not increase work effort. It appears that they were going in and out of welfare anyway and so did not respond to incentives. Or, they were too troubled or too handicapped to respond as was intended. Or, there were no jobs where they were, and so forth.

One important question cannot be answered by the study. MFIP cost the state from $1,900 to $3,800 more per family per year than AFDC had. There were great gains for some people and, arguably, for society, but would other states tolerate such costs? Would states be interested in an expensive program that helped working poor people but did not end, and, in fact, perpetuated, welfare? In 1998, Minnesota itself cut back on MFIP, lowering the level of income eligibility, providing less training, decreasing incentives, and introducing time limits. The MDRC study was conducted with a sample drawn before these program changes. In its report, MDRC cautions that its positive findings may not apply to the redesigned program.

SANCTIONS

Recipients all over the country who graduated from TANF to income from work alone or from work combined with assistance have received a good deal of attention, at least with regard to financial consequences for them. Gravely overlooked, however, are the consequences for applicants who have been "diverted" from assistance at intake and for recipients to whom so-called sanctions have been applied.

Sanctions are penalties for failure to comply with regulations. Failures range from a serious issue like refusing to look for work to merely missing an appointment with an i.m. worker, or, as in Colorado, neglecting to have a child vaccinated. Penalties are cash reductions in assistance and may be imposed for three or six months or indefinitely. They may be partial, as in canceling a parent's portion of a benefit while continuing the child's, or they may be sweeping, as in terminating all TANF payments. For details, see Appendix A, Table A–13. Either way, money available for the mother and child, who live as a family, after all, is reduced. Pause for a moment to ruminate about reducing cash available for a child's food or clothing in order to give the parent an incentive to have the child vaccinated.

The number of cases rejected at intake and the number sanctioned, taken together, exceed those regularly dealt with in the program. When this hidden clientele—silent majority, one might say—is pointed out to administrators, they tend, on the whole, to be cool. Many simply say that sanctions are necessary if TANF is to work and their assignment is to divert people from welfare, not to draw them in. Then how much in the way of sanctions relative to the service that is rendered is reasonable? The standard is, so far, hidden in the culture of welfare departments.

There is some difficulty in arriving at reasonable national statistics about sanctions. States use different definitions in collecting statistics; i.m. workers may report as voluntary a withdrawal that the client would regard as a sanction; and state statistics lump fully 56 percent of all closings under the classification "other"—a category that the 1998 HHS report obviously regards as suspect.

Trying to appraise the situation, *The Washington Post* reported in 1998 that "38 percent of those who left welfare during one three-month period last year did so because of state penalties."[9] In Florida, more than a quarter of the cases closed were a result of sanctions; in Indiana, more than half. At the end of 1999, *The New York Times* reported that 69 percent of home-relief clients in the city's workfare program had been sanctioned. Embarking on its welfare reform, called W-2, Wisconsin estimated that it would enroll 54,000 families, Instead, it enrolled only 13,000 families; by the end of 1999 the number had declined to 7,100. Who are the thousands who did not appear on, or disappeared from, W-2 rolls? Were they diverted at intake, sanctioned, or did they decide not to hang on until, inevitably, they would be dismissed?

In a March 2000 report, the U.S. General Accounting Office estimated that in an average month in 1998, 136,000 families were being sanctioned. According to limited studies that the office reviewed, their wages were lower than for those who had left TANF for other reasons. Asked about hardship, families reported that they could not pay bills, care for their children, or faced homelessness.[10]

Witnesses testifying to Congress on possible permutations of welfare reform occasionally pointed out, presumably with black humor, that the surest reform would be to close down the program entirely. One should not joke with earnest people. With the 1996 welfare reform, Congress intended to close down the program entirely; its most effective implements were not the training programs and incentives that were extensively discussed, but requirements for severe reductions in caseloads coupled with the administrative climate in welfare departments.

FOOD STAMPS AND MEDICAID

In the summer of 1999, President Clinton commented on a "piece of troubling news . . . a surprisingly large drop in the number of low income people receiving food stamps."[11] A drop of almost 30 percent from the 1996 figure, this was far more than had been anticipated when Congress deliberately cut back the program. About two-thirds of the families who left the program were still eligible for food stamps at the time that they left. In three short years from 1995 to 1998, the percentage of poor children who benefited from food stamps dropped from 88 percent to 70 percent.

There has been widespread unease and perplexity about this decline. In some measure, the perplexity arises from a tendency to regard poor people as cool maneuverers, without feeling or pride, who line up for whatever they can get. With welfare shrinking and low-tier wages stagnant, they should have flooded food stamp rolls, should they not?

In a survey about the effect of discontinuing daycare for welfare children in New York some years ago, interviewers came upon the fact that some mothers were not filing appeals that would—win or lose—give them an additional six months of daycare. Surveyors checked back to ask why the welfare mothers were not filing appeals and were told, in one way and another: "They want to get rid of us and they are going to get rid of us. The devil with them!" Similarly, as DeParle wrote in the article mentioned earlier: "Unwilling to work for a welfare check or endure more pointless classes, the poor voted with their feet. Most simply left."[12] Evidently, even poor people will tolerate only so much hassle and humiliation.

In any case, old-welfare, AFDC, had served as an effective intake device for food stamps. Frequently, AFDC recipients were automatically signed up for food stamps; at the very least, workers told them about it. Without AFDC, there is no automatic sign-up and many TANF workers fail simply to disclose that the families they deal with may be eligible for food stamps. In Ohio, for example, a TANF recipient who misses an appointment with a worker— maybe the woman is working and expects to be cut off, maybe she didn't get the message about the appointment, or whatever the reason—gets a letter from the state office saying she has been dropped. The letter says nothing about possible continued eligibility for TANF or Medicaid. In Ohio, 80 percent of those who left TANF were eligible for food stamps and Medicaid, but only half of these people received them.

When states and localities apply sanctions to TANF recipients, some also suspend or terminate food stamps, going "farther than the law permits in limiting benefits," the U.S. General Accounting Office drily reported.[13] The welfare reform law permits states to seek to waive the work requirement for food stamps in areas where the unemployment rate is over 10 percent. Twelve states have not applied for such a waiver, even though the Department of Agriculture judges that they would qualify for it.

Perhaps food stamp usage declines because not as many people need them? The U.S. Conference of Mayors reported an 18 percent increase across the country in requests for emergency food in 1999 and a 17 percent increase in 2000. Patterns of usage changed: there were more repeat customers, not just people seeking a one-time boost, and more working people. In response, hunger centers opened up for evening and weekend hours. In 1999, Congressman Tony Hall surveyed food banks and heard from 117 in forty states. Requests were up at 87 percent of them. Second Harvest, the nation's largest distributor of donated food, estimated that there would be a shortfall from 1997 to 2002 of the equivalent of three meals a day for three million people for an entire year. Almost all feeding centers attribute the increases in need for food at least partly to declining food stamp use.

Medicaid, the government program to provide health care for poor people, increased its coverage from 29 million in 1990 to 42 million in 1995. In 1996, the participation rate turned around so that 1.25 million fewer children had health care coverage by 1998. "This drop was primarily caused," says an Urban Institute report, "by sharp reductions in enrollment of adults and children receiving welfare."[14]

The decline, in the face of the growing number of people overall who were without health insurance, created even more anxiety and uncertainty than the issue about food stamps. For one thing, in enacting welfare reform, Congress had taken pains to provide that people who lose TANF would nevertheless continue to be eligible for Medicaid. In response to a presidential initiative, Congress had enacted a new program—the Children's Health Insurance Program (CHIP)—that would broaden coverage for poor children. So how could coverage decline?

Public discussion of the matter has a curious, though not unaccustomed, quality, focusing on the probable ignorance or negligence of poor families rather than on the institutions that are involved. As a result, considerable effort and sums of money are devoted to outreach, that is, efforts to educate poor people about the care that is available to them and urge them to use it. These efforts have some, but by no means adequate, effect.

A major source of the program lies in the behavior of welfare departments, that, as with food stamps, neglect to facilitate clients' access to health care. In many states, computer programs automatically dropped people from Medicaid when they lost welfare; despite the new legislation, the computer programs were not revised. Some states and localities took the position that their clients were *in*eligible for Medicaid. Thus, in 1999, only legal challenges led Pennsylvania to restore Medicaid to 32,000 former recipients. A suit on similar grounds was filed in Florida.

Apart from regulations that subvert the intent of law and the distanced attitude of welfare workers, arrangements that are ostensibly made to provide care operate against its use. Application and access are made difficult by limited hours of service, inconvenient location of offices, Medicaid practices that discourage physicians from taking Medicaid patients, and poor fit with the way people live.

With respect to this last point, for example, the CHIP program is available to children whose families meet low-income requirements, but not to their parents. Thus, a mother and child, both of whom have influenza, would be expected to go to one doctor for treatment of the child (which would be paid for by CHIP-Medicaid) and to some other doctor for the mother—the sick mother quite possibly schlepping the sick child across town on public transportation. In fact, the mother is more likely to go to an emergency room where she is accustomed to receive her own treatment and where the child will be treated as well—at much higher cost than in a physician's office, of course. In general, CHIP and Medicaid do not produce arrangements that bring to mind an entrepreneurial organization seeking market share.

Perhaps states withhold medical care because they are not able to pay for it? Congress provided $4.2 billion a year for CHIP for 1998 and 1999, but states spent $121 million in 1998 and just under $1 billion the next year. At the beginning of 2000, many states had not used up even their 1998 allotment. One must look elsewhere to understand the source of the states' problem in delivering care.

THE FAMILY AND CHILDREN

TANF assumed from AFDC a caseload that was largely limited to women who were single parents. It is, therefore, not surprising to learn that welfare women report that relationships with their men are often discouraging. Many have been abused or their children have been abused. Men may not be dependable, either in terms of relationship or of financial support. When asked, many welfare mothers say that they do not intend to marry. In part, they are concerned that it would be harder to leave a man to whom they are married and they think, based on prior experience and the experiences of family and friends, that there is some strong likelihood that it will come to that.

Or, they may express idealized views of marriage and say they intend to marry sometime, when they meet the right man, but they do not have high hopes of meeting him soon. For most, children are more important than a man and they will not risk the children's welfare. Kathryn Edin and others (1997) looked into these issues intimately with recipients in Philadelphia and Cleveland and report: "[Welfare mothers] viewed marriage in opposition to the need to take care of their children rather than as a means to do so. . . . Mothers sometimes reported that men (even those with whom they had had children) were jealous of their relationship with the children. . . . Virtually no mother we spoke to felt that they ought to marry for the sake of the children."[15]

Bearing these circumstances and attitudes in mind, as well as the crushing financial pressure that TANF mothers face, one may perhaps make sense out of the trickle of information that is available about the effect of welfare reform on the family arrangements of clients. However, it should be stipulated that research into this matter is extraordinarily difficult. That is, welfare families are characterized by change. They move in search of housing they can afford; they double up; a child goes to live with an aunt or grandmother; a parent works for a time and then loses a job. Distinguishing what would have happened in the family anyway from what happens after or because of welfare reform is a daunting task.

Still, it appears that welfare reform caused some families to lose their homes. Because low-income housing is in such short supply, almost 40 percent of working poor families spend more than half of their income on housing. A family graduates from TANF to work and, after several months, the mother loses her job. The very first crisis the family faces is not being able to pay the rent. Mother and children are evicted and enter the spiral of losing furnishings, moving in with relatives, moving on to friends, placing one child or another with an aunt or grandmother, and eventually entering an emergency shelter. Even though the mother finds another job, low-paid, to be sure, establishing oneself in an apartment takes more money than can readily be assembled.

According to the U.S. Conference of Mayors, requests for emergency shelter by families rose 15 percent in the year 2000[16]— a period of high prosperity. Shelter workers generally agree that welfare reform is a major factor in this rise. Homeless families with children were unusual not so many years ago; by 1998, 40 percent of homeless families included children—well over one million children during the year. Policies in New York State applying TANF work requirements and sanctions to families with children in shelters resulted in their deliberate expulsion from the shelters. Having been homeless as a child is a predictor of being homeless as an adult, observed Martha Burt of the Urban Institute in connection with one report, "so you're building the next generation there to an alarming extent."[17]

It is not surprising, then, that welfare reform has produced an increase in the number of children in state or county-operated foster homes. The number of children in foster care has been rising steadily for some years for other reasons, but a report on Wisconsin's W-2 program, for example, notes that 5 percent of mothers forced off welfare and into low-wage jobs have had to "abandon their children."[18] A study in Utah concluded that one-half of TANF recipients who were sanctioned wound up involved with child welfare authorities. According to studies by Kathleen Wells and Shenyang Guo at Case Western Reserve University, and by Peter Brandon of the University of Massachusetts, when families lose welfare, or benefits are reduced, the likelihood of a mother's separation from her child increases.

TANF families may have recourse to grandparents for various services—for daycare while the mother works, because the mother simply cannot manage, or because the family has been sanctioned—but the children can receive TANF if a grandparent cares for them. The steady growth in the number of TANF cases in which only a child and no parent is supported (23 percent of all cases in 1999) reflects increasing care by grandparents or other relatives. Grandparents have troubles of their own, of course; the typical parent of a woman receiving welfare is not well off either.

It is a novel and an unexpected finding of recent studies that care by relatives is not, in general, superior to the dubious care offered in most organized settings. This seems to mean that aunts or grandparents are now so stressed themselves that they take a child because the situation of the child and the child's mother is even more desperate than their own—the overwhelming fear, of course, is that the "county" will take the child. So the relatives, reluctantly, take the child.

TANF recipients who have settled into work with some degree of success frequently say that their children are proud of them—obviously, the mothers are pleased about this—and that they are setting a good example for their children. Mothers (some of them the same women) also express anxiety about not being able to supervise their children as well as they should. An occasional study—this is all there is—speaks of maternal depression and unbearable stress.[19]

There are anecdotal reports of women finally taking into their homes men whom they have been fending off. They thought them risky, in terms of abuse or for other reasons. With TANF income lost or diminished and the mother required to fulfill a work requirement, however, the men offer financial support and help with child care that the mothers cannot decline. No one knows how many mothers make these trade-offs because of TANF. It is plausible that some do—women make considerable sacrifices for their children—but how is one really to know?

I observe in passing that it has become customary to talk about low-income people as having a "culture" that accounts for the disordered way they live, but much of what is seen as "cultural" is composed of such triage-like strategies as have been indicated.

THE MERIT SYSTEM AND STATEWIDENESS

The Social Security Act, establishing ADC so many years ago, required states to establish a merit system for employing welfare workers and to apply every provision of its welfare law in every jurisdiction of the state. The first provision was an attempt, successful in some large measure, as it turned out, to avoid the nepotism and patronage that were widespread in the states. The second provision was an attempt, also largely successful, to keep state governments from favoring one section of a state over another or some counties over others (think of urban county–rural county jockeying for advantage, for example).

TANF wiped out these provisions and there has not so far been time for well-established institutional arrangements to change. Nothing now prevents states from lapsing into former patterns again, however.

WHERE ARE THEY . . .

In Chapter 1, we asked: "Where are they, the people who are suffering?"

They are at feeding centers; they are homeless on the streets, in shelters, or crowded into the homes of families that cannot turn them away. They are children in and out of foster homes who feel shoved about; they are parents and children who do not eat regularly or properly; they are anxious and driven. They are fractured families, fractured by government regulations; they are children who cannot learn because they do not sleep; they are family members struggling to protect a frail parent or a mentally ill sister in spare time that is never available.

Empathy is the most human of qualities. Anyone who looks straight at others and thinks how their lives seem to them will know where they are.

TANF is a mean program, mean in design and meanly administered. It spreads pain and mischief and it will not achieve any decent national purpose at reasonable social cost.

NOTES

1. Pamela Loprest, "How Families that Left Welfare Are Doing: A National Picture." The Urban Institute: Washington, D.C., 1999. P. 4

2. Jason DeParle, "Bold Effort Leaves Much Unchanged for the Poor." *New York Times*, December 30, 1999. P. 12.

3. "Turning the Needy Away." *New York Times*, Editorial Page, July 31, 2000.

4. Laura Leete, Neil Bania, and Claudia Coulton, "Automobile Access and Public Transit among Welfare Recipients," Center on Poverty and Social Change, Briefing Report no. 9905. Cleveland, OH: Case Western Reserve University, 1999.

5. Sheila R. Zedlewski, "Work Activity and Obstacles to Work Among TANF Recipients." The Urban Institute: Washington, D.C., 1999.

6. Op. Cit., p. 1.

7. Katherine S. Newman, *No Shame in My Game: The Working Poor in the Inner City*. Russell Sage Foundation/Knopf: New York, 1999. Preface, p. xiv.

8. Virginia Knox, Cynthia Miller and Lisa A. Gennetian. *Reforming Welfare and Rewarding Work: A Summary of the Final Report on the Minnesota Family Investment Program*. Manpower Demonstration Research Corporation: New York. September 2000. And personal letter from Cynthia Miller, July 14, 2000.

9. "State Sanctions Contribute to Dropping Welfare Rolls." *Washington Post Report*, March 23, 1998.

10. U.S. General Accounting 8TB Office, *Welfare Reforms: State Sanctions Policies and Number of Families Affected*, GAO/HEHS-00-44, March 31, 2000. See also copy of letter from Cynthia M. Fagnoni to Senator Daniel Patrick Moynihan, dated June 14, 2000, reproduced in GAO/HEHS-00-133R, pp. 1–2. The letter responds to further detailed questions from Senator Moynihan.

11. "Study Says Welfare Changes Made the Poorest Worse Off." *New York Times*, August 23, 1999. P. A13.

12. Jason DeParle op.cit.

13. "Food Stamp Program: Various Factors Have Led to Declining Participation." *Month in Review*, August 1999. GAO: Washington, D.C. P. 41.

14. Leighton Ku and Brian Bruen, "The Continuing Decline in Medicaid Coverage." The Urban Institute, 1999. P. 5.

15. Kathryn Edin, Ellen K. Scott, Andrew S. London and Joan Maya Mazelis, "My Children Come First: Welfare-Reliant Women's Post-TANF Views of Work-Family Tradeoffs, Neighborhoods, and Marriage." Paper presented at the Northwestern University/University of Chicago Joint Center for Poverty Research conference. Washington, D.C., September 16–17, 1999.

16. U.S. Conference of Mayors, *States Report of Hunger and Homelessness in Surveyed Cities in 2000*, Washington, D.C., December 2000. P. 38.

17. Quoted in Nina Bernstein, "Study Documents Homelessness in American Children Each Year." *New York Times*, February 1, 2000. P. A12. For a more extensive statement, relating homelessness to welfare reform, see Martha Burt, Laudan Aron, Edgar Lee, and Jesse Valente, *America's Homeless: Temporary Shelter vs. Affordable Housing*, Chapter 11. The Urban Institute: Washington D.C., 2001.

18. Jason DeParle, "A Welfare Plan Justifies Hopes and Some Fear." *New York Times*, January 15, 1999. P. 1.

19. For example, see Eileen P. Sweeney, "Recent Studies Indicate that Many Parents Who Are Current or Former Welfare Recipients Have Disabilities or Other Medical Conditions," Center on Budget and Policy Priorities, Washington, D.C., February 29, 2000. Pp. 2–3.

Chapter Five

Mothers, Children, and Work

In the last pages of Chapter 4, we reviewed what might reasonably be said about the direct impact of welfare reform on children and their families. Some children are better off; they are proud of their working mother and it is said that they will follow her example. A comparatively few families, their children included, of course, have more total income than when they received cash assistance.

Yet, as a result of welfare reform, many children are moved about—arbitrarily, as it seems to them, aimlessly—into daycare; from their mother to a grandmother; to a county foster home, and, with luck, back home again; from one school to another or to no school at all; even into the street or to a shelter for the homeless. They may not eat as well as they once did; they may be deprived of medical care. Viewed educationally, it is as if they were being schooled to become poor adults—untrained, insecure, truculent.

This is not to say that ADC was a good program for children, of course, but only that TANF or no assistance at all is worse.

If we are to proceed beyond criticism to framing better policies, it is necessary to confront the premises of welfare reform. The quintessential premise—unquestioned by hardly anyone these days—is that everyone must work. However, insistence on universal work is in serious conflict with concern for children, and it not a snug fit with family values either. This is a problem.

In what follows, there is no intent to question whether work is important for people. Savants ranging from Karl Marx to Alan Greenspan have asserted that work is central to people's lives, so who will differ? Even apart from income, most people *need* paid work—to organize their time, to gain or retain status, for social contact, and so forth. Scholars who have looked closely at the matter testify to this need.

Still, it is not clear that *everyone* needs paid work *at all times*. For example, until recently, an ever-increasing proportion of workers, not all of them elderly, was retiring voluntarily—without discernible distress. And a moment's thought brings to mind several kinds of young adults who adjust well or even better without paid work; for example, the partners of well-to-do spouses and the married mothers and, in fewer cases, the married fathers of young children.

This leads to a first observation about the American work ethic: our society does not require work from spouses of the well-to-do or from pensioned people who can retire to a country club development in Florida. No one even complains about them. So why is it okay to draw social security while one swims in the ocean or plays bridge or poker, but it is not okay to receive TANF while one attends college? This question is raised now only to say that, plainly, our devotion to the work ethic is subject to qualification.

A SCHIZOID POLICY

Why do we not qualify this devotion with respect to the care of young children? We have practiced a schizoid policy in the United States in recent years, emphasizing the importance of personal attention to a child by a mother or parent, on one hand, and forcing young mothers into the labor force, on the other hand.

We have had a stream of scientific reports about the development of a child's brain during the child's first three years, emphasizing the critical role that the parents' personal attention plays in stimulating the organization of the circuitry in the baby's brain. These studies seem to say that, once missed, the opportunity for optimum intellectual development cannot be renewed. This is not an observation that affects only poor children or poor parents. Half of *all* women with year-old babies are in the workforce; most of these women returned to work before their babies were six months old.

After the appearance of the Carnegie Commission report (1994),[1] on which the observations just above were based, President Bill Clinton spoke in his State of the Union message about the need to nurture children from the first days of their lives. The 1997 National Governor's Association Convention devoted itself to early childhood development, and there was much media attention.

A couple of years later, Dr. Sarah Blaffer Hrdy published a well-regarded book about the infant-mother bond over the millennia, considered from the point of view of evolutionary biology. She concluded that a human baby needs constant, attentive care, which is best provided by the child's mother or in daycare of a quality not readily available. Assuring this care, she wrote urgently, is essential to "the future of the human race, and the future of the planet."[2]

Other experts reacted powerfully against this view that "early is forever."[3] For example, a book called *The Myth of the First Three Years* maintains that the brain develops throughout life; its structure responds continuously to experience. Early deprivation, it says, can at least sometimes be compensated for and nurturing young children does not and should not preclude help to older children and adults.

Thus, a balanced view would recognize that personal attention to youngsters, especially early eye-to-eye contact with infants and all that goes with it, though not always irreplaceable, is vitally important to children's development and maturation.

More or less as the president was speaking and the governors were meeting, however, they and practically everyone else were engaged in reforming welfare, that is, in requiring that mothers of young children be occupied at work or in activities that would lead to work. It is baffling to consider how one can pursue these two objectives simultaneously. So far, well over a million toddlers and babies are in child care because of welfare reform.

In the course of working out welfare reform, there was much talk about expanding daycare for children. In contrast with earlier welfare reforms, there appears actually to have been some expansion. However, the quality of daycare that is generally available is far below the standard that the Carnegie Commission report or Dr. Hrdy would suggest. The care that infants and toddlers receive, the report said, is "of such substandard quality that it adversely affects [their] development."[4]

Surveys confirm this statement, using terms such as "poor to mediocre" and "hazardous" about the quality of daycare. For example, a national study by the Families and Work Institute in New York dealt with care in the homes of relatives and others. More than one-third of the arrangements were called "inadequate (growth harming)." Only 9 percent were rated "good"; half the children had "anxious/avoidant" or "anxious/resistant" relationships with their teachers.[5] These two terms mean, for example, that a one-year-old who fell down would not turn to a teacher to be comforted; if picked up, the child would become rigid or fight to be set down.

A recent, extensive study in California, Connecticut, and Florida concluded that many children in daycare spent their time watching television or wandering aimlessly around the room. They were retarded in language and social development and had little interaction with the workers who were caring for them.[6]

To make matters worse, an Urban Institute study shows that in order to adapt to their schedules, most mothers juggle multiple child-care arrangements, using a combination of congregate centers, babysitting by relatives and friends, or other arrangements.[7] One-third of parents with young children in the country (this from another Families and Work Institute study) work an early morning, a late night, or a split shift.[8] One-third of one- and two-year-olds receive two or more kinds of care while the mother works. Such numbers give a sense of the strain and constant adjustment for mothers as well as for children.[9]

Other studies suggest that children *can* receive good daycare.[10] With luck and more money than poor people have, it is possible to receive good care, so-called developmental daycare. However, this has little to do with what happens to most children. In any event, in the face of a nationwide shortage of daycare and the pressure of welfare reform, it appears that states are increasingly turning to unlicensed and unregulated care, so even the level of care we have now will deteriorate.

Is it clear what social purpose is served? We press mothers to work (at low wages), handing over their children to other people for care (at low wages), even though that care is likely to harm the children and undermine their development. How does a mother, a child, or our society benefit from this?

WORKING-CLASS AND MIDDLE-INCOME FAMILIES

Although not as directly as with parents who are involved with welfare reform, our social arrangements compel almost all parents to work, notably because two parents need to work if they are to pay their bills. For many years, the minimum wage would meet the poverty-level needs of a family of four—if an adult worked a full year at that wage. Industry paid a "family wage," it was said. Today, an adult working full-time all year at minimum wage barely earns poverty-level income for a family of two.

A study by the Annie E. Casey Foundation estimated that in 1969, the percentage of men twenty-five to thirty-four years old—the prime child-rearing years—who earned less than the amount needed to lift a family of four above the poverty level was 13.6 percent. By 1993, at 32.2 percent, the percentage had more than doubled.[11] Thus, in 1997 about 15 million people, including 8.7 million children, lived in so-called working-poor families.

Never mind the minimum wage and the government-defined poverty level. Higher, although still moderate, wages eroded roughly in tandem with the erosion of the minimum wage, as many economists would expect. In the decade ending in 1973, nearly every worker's income grew by about 25 percent in real (inflation-adjusted) money. That was the turnaround year; between 1973 and 1995, real wages at the low end of the scale fell by 22 percent! For middle-range workers earning about $25,000 a year, real wages declined by 10 percent.[12] For example, between 1993 and 2000, the number of jobs in New York City paying less than $25,000 a year climbed 22%, nearly four times as fast as jobs paying $25,000 to $75,000.[13]

In a book called *Illusions of Opportunity*, political scientist John Schwarz offers $27,000 a year as the income necessary to maintain a minimally adequate standard of living for a family of four.[14] It is hard to imagine that a family would be satisfied with $25,000, or $27,000, for that matter, or would feel that it could get by, but Schwarz estimated that 16 million jobs did not pay even this much. So if there are two parents in the home, both must work.

To add to the stress in families when both partners must work, Americans are now working longer hours. Americans once reacted to earning more income by taking more leisure. The average number of hours worked in a week declined from the 1960s to 1982; since then, year by year, the number of hours has been going up.[15] Labor department surveys find that from 1995 through 1998, middle-income family members added 70 hours a year, on average, to their work time, or nearly 1.8 million additional weeks in total. (There is a view that more hours of work for the same pay accounts, in considerable part, for reports of increased productivity that buoyed up stock market indices for a while.) Thus, two working parents have even less time away from work, that is, less time available for their children, than they would have had two decades ago.

In short, whether by direct instruction by welfare officials or from the financial pressures of the American wage structure, parents in all types of American families find that they must work, and they work longer hours. The issue raised here concerns mothers most directly and is not whether they may work or should be discouraged from working; it is whether they *must* work, however they feel about it. If not, we need to consider how—whether by wages or by government programming—we can support reasonable incomes for young families in which only one adult works. Since this book is about welfare reform, the narrowest question is whether it ought to be policy for such a program to require the mother of a young child to work, regardless of her circumstances and no matter how she feels about it. Taking into account the advice that has emerged from the studies of experts and the evidence that TANF provides of the consequences of such a policy, one would think that the answer would be, at the least, "no, certainly not every mother."

NOTES

1. *Starting Points: Meeting the Needs of Our Youngest Children.* New York: Carnegie Corporation, 1994.

2. Sarah Blaffer Hrdy. *Mother Nature: A History of Mothers, Infants, and Natural Selection.* Pantheon Books, 1999. The quotation is from an interview by Natalie Angier in "Primate Expert Explores Motherhood's Brutal Side." *New York Times*, February 8, 2000. P. Science-1.

3. So characterized in Jerome Bruner, "Tot Thought." *New York Review*, March 9, 2000. P. 27.

4. Carnegie Corporation, op. cit.

5. Reported in Joe Sexton, "Growth of Informal Child Care for New York Welfare Mothers Stirs Questions." *New York Times*, March 14, 1996. See also *Families and Work Institute*, New York, 1994.

6. Tamar Lewin, "Study Finds Welfare Changes Lead a Million Children into Child Care." *New York Times*, February 4, 2000.

7. Jeffrey Capizzano and Gina Adams, "The Number of Child Care Arrangements Used by Children Under Five: Variation Across States," The Urban Institute, number B–12. Washington, D.C. March 2000.

8. Sarah Kershaw, "Day Care at Night? New York Lags Behind." *New York Times*, April 2, 2000.

9. Karen Gullo, "Parents Juggle Child Care Arrangements." *Plain Dealer*, March 8, 2000.

10. Duane Alexander, director of the National Institute of Child Health: "The most striking aspect of these results from the early child-care study is that children are not being placed at a disadvantage in terms of cognitive development *if they have high-quality care in their first three years*" (emphasis added). Quoted in "A New Study of Day Care Shows Benefit of Attention." *New York Times*, April 5, 1997.

11. Steven A. Holmes, "Low-Wage Fathers and the Welfare Debate." *New York Times*, April 25, 1995.

12. Louis Uchitelle, "Strike Points to Inequalities in a Two-Tier Labor Market." *New York Times*, August 8, 1997.

13. Steven Greenhouse, "Low-Paid Jobs Lead Advance in Employment." *New York Times*, October 1, 2000.

14. John E. Schwarz, *Illusions of Opportunity: The American Dream in Question*. W. W. Norton, New York, 1997.

15. Juliet B. Schor, *The Overworked American: The Unexpected Decline of Leisure*. Basic Books, New York, 1991.

Chapter Six

Poverty's Three Constant Companions

Premises other than whether everyone must work at all times need to be reconsidered. Here, we discuss premises about how poverty is defined and about how American income should be shared.

POVERTY

The definition of poverty that we use today was devised in the early 1960s by Mollie Orshansky, an economist with the Social Security Administration. Reasoning that a minimally nutritious diet is the most primitive necessity, she multiplied the cost of such a diet by three—a number distilled from research on family consumption patterns—to arrive at the poverty level. Because the cost of a *routine* minimally nutritious diet would have produced a much larger, politically incorrect number of poor people, Orshansky relied in devising her definition on the Department of Agriculture's less expensive *emergency* diet—a diet meant to be used for only a brief period of time.

Apart from an annual correction to take account of the cost of living, this definition has remained basically unchanged for forty years. In that time, however, consumption patterns have changed considerably; families now spend a far smaller proportion of their income on food. With food stamps, Medicaid, and other so-called in-kind programs not yet enacted, Orshansky's definition was based on cash income alone, but today, in-kind income is very important to poor people. The early definition represented about half of median family income, but this proportion has now declined to about 40 percent. Because of these and other changes, the government is seriously considering proposals to revise the definition of poverty.

When it was launched, the official poverty level already understated genuine minimum needs, as its roots in an emergency diet suggest. It strains credulity to believe that the current (2000) level—$14,150 for a family of three and $17,050 for a family of four—represents minimum adequacy. As early as 1978, Orshansky herself recommended a more reasonable level. One indication that the current poverty level has come to seem too low is that new legislation targeting poor people regularly sets higher eligibility limits—135 percent of the poverty level, 150 percent, 200 percent. The public's estimate of the minimum income that a family would require varies, surveys indicate, from $20,000 to almost $30,000 a year.

WELFARE POVERTY/WORKER POVERTY

Living below the poverty level is a day-to-day reality, not only for welfare clients, but for the 15 million adults and children in working poor families as well. Although we tend to think of welfare clients as distinct from the working poor, in fact there is considerable overlap.

Even before welfare reform, half of all applications for assistance were connected with a family member's loss of a job or of hours of work. That is, half of all applicants were in the labor force before they found that they had to resort to welfare. Many clients worked while receiving welfare, sometimes reporting their income as was required and sometimes not. Clients frequently left welfare to take a job; frequently, too, they returned to seek welfare when they lost a job.

The relationship is even tighter than the back-and-forth of work and welfare suggests. As Katherine Newman writes in *No Shame in My Game*, "Rather than paint welfare and work as different worlds, it makes far more sense to describe them as two halves of a single coin, as an integrated economic system at the very bottom of our social structure."

"Kyesha's family," Newman writes, "is a clear exampleof this fusion. Her mother needs the income her working child brings into the house; Kyesha needs the subsidies (housing, medical care, etc.) that state aid provides to her mother. Only because the two domains are linked can this family manage to make ends meet, and then just barely."[1] A grandmother caring for a child who receives TANF while the mother, in a separate household, works and contributes to the support of the two of them is not uncommon, especially after welfare reform.

As one learns more about the pool of working-poor population from which welfare draws its clients, one perceives that TANF does not so much upgrade the earning capacity of welfare clients as it privatizes public welfare—shifting dependent families horizontally from parsimonious government support to parsimonious employer wages.

Just to remind ourselves what less-than-poverty-level income can mean: missed meals, doubling up and crowding, homelessness, unremitting stress, overflow of pressures to family members and friends who may be poorly equipped to handle them, and children farmed out.

Thus, the inability of so many people—on and off welfare—to achieve poverty-level income is, to be sure, a measure of the profound failure of both the American wage structure and government programs like TANF and EITC. But merely reaching the 1960 standard—widely understood to be grossly inadequate—in the wealthy, radically changed world of 2000 and onward would be small reason to celebrate. We must reach higher.

FAIR SHARES

We are accustomed to think of income in terms of established sums—a teacher's salary, income from renting a house, interest from a savings certificate—as if these were absolute values. Viewed differently, however, wages, rent, and interest simply serve to divide up the nation's goods and services. "I have ten claims on the country's million units of goods, you have eight claims" and so forth. The validity of this view becomes plain in inflationary times, when what I earn or pay for an item becomes meaningful only in relation to what you earn or pay.

The division of claims that results always seems imperfect. In the end, we apply correctives like preferences and graduated rates to the income tax system and pay out money through social security and other so-called cash transfers like the EITC. The tax and transfer systems have other purposes as well but altering disparities is one. An attempt to arrive at fairer shares is also implicit in minimum wage and prevailing wage legislation and other legislation intended to raise the income of some kinds of people relative to others.

How, finally, to define fair shares is the stuff of arguments generally conducted at a high level of abstraction or a low level of self-interest. At one extreme is a formulation in a 1971 book by philosopher John Rawls called *A Theory of Justice*: "All goods are to be distributed equally unless an unequal distribution of any or all of these goods is to the advantage of the least favored."[2]

At the other extreme is the view held by many economists that, when least interfered with, self-interest and the private market provide the most for everyone, including the disadvantaged.

Over the years, economists and most others find a pragmatic position somewhere between these extremes. A compromise position on inequality is worked out in the public arena, where it is a shifting vector of conscience, unrest, and economic and political power. In the glory days of the welfare state after the Second World War, it was widely thought that the government should aim at reducing inequality. There was much debate about the goal of equality, even at that more idealistic time. In time, a less ambitious, less controversial goal came to be accepted: assured provision to all of minimum levels of food, housing, health care, and so forth. Although this was the commonly stated goal, preferences still proliferated, some explicit and public, and a great many that were more or less invisible.

As the matter would otherwise have been hopelessly involved, reporting about inequality rested on cash income alone. The best known indicator was, and is, the proportion of cash national income that goes to the poorest fifth of the population, to the next fifth, and to the third, fourth, and fifth (the richest) fifths. The rest of this section documents a radical increase in inequality in the United States in the past quarter of a century. For example, in 1980, according to *The Wall Street Journal*, CEOs earned 42 times as much as their line employees; in 1998, they earned 419 times as much.

The share of income of the poorest 20 percent (the lowest fifth) averaged around 5 percent for the thirty years from the great Depression to the 1970s. Full employment and government controls during World War II brought their share up modestly; after the war, it fell back. The civil rights movement and the war against poverty produced a blip upward, soon gone from the screen. In the 1980s, the share of the poorest fifth began a sustained decline. In a single legislative act in 1981, President Ronald Reagan's first budget produced a drop of 0.2 percent in the share of the poorest fifth of the population and an increase of 0.9 percent for the richest fifth.

The cumulative effect of government policy and the economy after 1981 was to drop the share of the poorest fifth of the population from 5.2 to 4.2 percent by 1999. These are small numbers, but they indicate a precipitous 20 percent decline. As one may surmise, simultaneously the share of the richest fifth increased—from 41 to 47 percent. See Appendix A, Tables A–27 to A–45. The richest fifth of the population had as much income in 1999 as all the rest of the population taken together.[3]

One might think that, riding the coattails of the rich, the middle-class gained at least a little? Not so. They did not prosper. In this period, all fifths except the richest fifth lost some portion of their share.

As for wealth (the value of land, homes, buildings, businesses, stocks, and bonds) in this period, the net wealth of all but the wealthiest families had *declined*, despite all the talk about the spread of investment in the stock market. Indeed, there is some alarm about the increasing burden of debt that poor and middle-class families are assuming. As for the top 20 percent, by 1995 they held 84 percent of all national wealth.

THE CONSTANT COMPANIONS

Low wages, penurious welfare, and a markedly inferior share of income for the lowest fifth appear together, on scene or off, whenever poverty is at issue. They are the constant companions of poverty.

Almost any problem can force already poor people to turn from the work they are doing or have lost to welfare, if it is at all available, of course. Reciprocally, welfare offers such a miserable alternative to work that people wearily turn back to the labor market, even without a formal requirement that they do so. As income from work and welfare ratchet down, increments of shares flow upward toward the top of the income distribution. Put more plainly, as wages and welfare levels decline, profits become higher and tax levels lower.

Many dispute this view, offering one or another variant of "a rising tide lifts all ships," but painstaking analysis in an Economic Policy Institute book called *The State of Working America, 1998–99*, by Lawrence Mishel, Jared Bernstein, and John Schmitt (1999), supports these assertions. Family income, the analysis notes, depends heavily on whether the income is derived from work, from proceeds from capital such as interest and capital gains, or from government payments. In the roughly two decades from 1979 to 1997, income from capital has increased as a percentage of all income in the United States (from 16.1 percent to 20.4 percent). Obviously, this favors those who are better off. Simultaneously, income from work has declined as a percentage (from 74 percent to 70.7 percent), exacting a cost from those who are relatively poorer.

If wages and salaries commanded the same share of national income today as in 1979, the authors write, hourly compensation would be 5.4 percent higher, a more than 50 percent increase over the actual growth from 1979 to 1996.

Although he handles the statistics somewhat differently, Edward N. Wolff, a New York University economist, arrives at a similar conclusion about the relation of profits and wages. In 1965, he he writes, labor began gaining a larger share of business revenue at the expense of profits. By the end of the 1970s, however, profit started to regain its lost share, winding up with an all-time high share by the beginning of 1998.

In short, low wages are closely tied to, if not actually created by, all-time high profits and both are reflected in the markedly uneven distribution of income. Low wages set a ceiling for welfare benefits and the border between low wages and welfare is as permeable in both directions as Mexico's border is with the United States. Thus, welfare levels are also inversely tied to profits and to the distribution of income.

WHY SHOULD WE CARE ABOUT THIS CONSTANT RELATIONSHIP?

The question is posed because some think, and a few write, that low wages, penurious welfare, and a markedly inferior share of income for the lowest fifth of the population are the natural order and have salutary effects: they serve to correct the character of the slothful, they reward the energetic and imaginative, and they provide an incentive for self-improvement. Proof, the argument goes, lies in the remarkable social mobility of American society—equal opportunity operating as it is intended to operate.

A recent study called "By Our Own Bootstraps" for the Federal Reserve Board—a strikingly misleading study—is offered in evidence. It shows that only 5 percent of the poorest fifth remain in the lowest income group over a seventeen-year period of time. However, this study counts students and other youths from high-income families as upwardly mobile when, in time, they take full-time jobs. One hopes that the country's fiscal policies are based on better studies that this.

More careful studies that have been conducted in recent years do not bear out the assumption of a fluid, mobile society. Peter Gottschalk and Sheldon Danziger, professors at Boston College and the University of Michigan, examined the fate of children during the 1970s and 1980s. Almost nine out of ten in the bottom fifth remained in the bottom two-fifths ten and twenty years later. Another study, by Samuel Bowles and Herbert Gintis, found that "of 1,000 children born into the bottom tenth of incomes only four will make it to the top tenth."[4]

Generally speaking, born poor means live poor. We may be born equal but it is into an unequal world. That the bottom fifth is heavily populated by women, especially women with children, blacks, and other minorities creates the appearance of a caste society, an idea foreign to our democratic view of ourselves. Still, at the intersection of class and ethnicity or gender is where caste may be found. This is a problem created by the three constant companions and we cannot turn our backs on it. Nor, in a wealthy country, can so many people be consigned to this fate for no good reason.

Would a more equitable distribution of income interfere with equality of opportunity? It does not seem so. The United States does not have more social mobility than European countries like Germany and Sweden, which have extensive, redistributive safety nets and far more equity.

PRACTICAL BENEFITS OF FAIR SHARES

There are substantial practical reasons to correct such seriously inequitable shares, including greatly reducing the number who are poor, providing a fair break in the marketplace for the purchasing power of lower-income people, lengthening the life span and improving the health of all Americans, and preventing social unrest. A few words should be said about each.

Reducing Poverty

This is what we have been discussing. A fairer share would leave room for more decent, if still comparatively lower, wages. Depending on the wage levels, many or most workers would not be poor. This would leave room for a decent standard of income support for families without income from work that the nation may want to support.

Less poverty would mean a society with less distress, fewer troubled children and parents, more stable families, less crime and delinquency and, undoubtedly, less mental illness. And it would mean a society with less free-floating resentment (see the discussions of "relative deprivation" under "Better Health for All" and "Social Unrest" below).

A Fair Break in the Marketplace

Supply and demand is not entirely a simple principle. Producers and merchandisers do not respond only to the money in a consumer's hand; they act also on judgments about the *aggregation of customers* from whom they can earn the most. They are drawn by customers or markets with large sums to spend and they vacate markets where there is little money (unless, of course, they can charge disproportionately more).

Just as television networks do not provide much adult, sophisticated programming because audiences of a few million do not provide the "market share" they seek, so, for example, do home builders move up the scale to high-cost homes if there is a market for them, vacating the production of low-income housing even though there would be customers for it.

Every year there are more "struggling renter households," as the U.S. Department of Housing and Urban Development (HUD) calls very low-income families that rent, but the number of rental units they might be able to afford decreased by 372,000 between 1991 and 1997. "The sad truth," HUD Secretary Andrew Cuomo observed, "is that more and more people working at low-wage jobs . . . are being priced out of the housing market as rents rise."[5]

Why, contrary to what we glean about economics from talk shows, does supply wane even as the market waxes? These buildings are worth more for other purposes—up-scale housing or commercial uses—and landlords charge rents they think they can get or sell them off. This is also true with respect to purchased housing. As better-off people have more money to spend, the average new home becomes more luxurious and larger—50 percent larger than in 1970. Moderate-income people cannot afford them and fewer more modestly priced homes are built.

In short, the flood of money into higher incomes commandeers housing construction; as a result, homes for rent or for purchase at modest cost become hard to find. As middle-income people know very well, relatively few adult children now can buy "starter" houses without help from parents, as young adult children once did.

It hardly needs to be said that the quality of housing often determines other important issues—the quality of schools for one's children, the safety and congeniality of the neighborhood in which one lives. Retail stores withdraw from depressed neighborhoods and yet, ironically, prices rise relative to the prices in more expensive areas. Just as the very rich withdraw into gated communities, the poor and the "struggling middle-class" (to adapt HUD's term) find themselves ghettoized—not necessarily what they would have wanted.

Housing is but one example of the wealth-induced withdrawal of business from lower-cost consumer goods. Auto manufacturers embellish and enlarge their cars every year and phase out low-cost models. Low-cost, low-maintenance, basic telephone service evaporates as communication companies provide new and better services for the majority who can or will pay for them. Banks specialize in creative fee charging for small accounts. Household appliances are computerized, making them more expensive; cheaper, unimproved appliances are hard to come by. Public services like museums and recreation facilities, once free, charge fees to support the higher level of service they render.

This is all to say that, in the aggregate, lower- and moderate-income people deploy so little purchasing power *in comparison to* the money now in the hands of upper-middle-class and rich people that they cannot find what they want in the market, or they have to pay more for it. This is not fair, to be sure, but it is also of practical moment to people with moderate or lower incomes.

Better Health for All

A steady stream of research in Britain, Canada, and the United States appears to demonstrate that inequality *causes* high rates of ill health and shortens life expectancy. This is not a question of whether more poor people means more poor health, an idea we may be prepared to accept, but of the way income is spread about within a society. One does not arrive easily at the conclusion that *everyone's* health is governed, in some measure, by the distribution of income; the conclusion is driven by the research of physicians, economists, and sociologists.

For example, the highest life expectancies in the developed world are in countries, like Japan and Sweden, that have very low ratios of inequality, according to the United Nations Development Report for 1999. Their citizens live two or three years longer, on the average, than in the United States and Britain, which have the highest ratios of inequality in the developed worlds.[6] Similarly, states such as New York and Louisiana, which have the nation's most unequal incomes have higher early death rates than states such as Utah and Minnesota. One recognizes in these examples that the absolute wealth of a country or state does not, in itself, produce good health. Something else is operating.

In 1998, the *American Journal of Public Health* published a study of 282 metropolitan areas in the United States that found that mortality rates are more closely linked to relative than to absolute income. "What do Biloxi, Miss., Las Cruces, N.M. and Steubenville, Ohio, have in common?" a report of the study asks. And replies: "High inequality, high mortality. Allentown, Pa., Pittsfield, Mass., and Milwaukee? Low inequality. Low mortality."[7]

Christopher Jencks, a sociologist at Harvard, put it like this for *The New York Times*: "The data seem to say that if you are of average income, living among people of average income, you are less likely to have a heart attack than if you live more stressfully in a community where there is you in the middle, and a bunch of rich people and a bunch of poor people. That seems hard to believe but it is the direction in which the evidence seems to point."[8]

A study by Harriet Orcutt Duleep published in the *Social Security Bulletin* in 1995 sums it up even more crisply. "The income distribution of a nation is an important determinant of its mortality," she writes. "The relatively unequal distribution of income in the United States is an important contributing factor to its low life expectancy."[9]

Speculation about the link between health and inequality focuses on the sense of community or neighborliness that may be characteristic of countries or regions with relatively low inequality. Stress, induced by a sense of "relative deprivation" (see below) that flows from great inequality, has also figured prominently among theories, especially as medical interest in stress has deepened.

Whatever the explanation, the moral seems to be that it is in the healthy self-interest of the relatively well-to-do share, one way or another, with those who are less prosperous.

Social Unrest

A classic study by W.G. Runciman in 1966 suggests two conditions that may, in particular, lead to a sense of relative deprivation or grievance. One is a person's position relative to others: How far removed does one perceive oneself from others with whom one makes comparison? Second is a person's state of expectation: How does one judge the chance or likelihood of self-improvement? A larger gap in relative positions and higher expectations tends to magnify a sense of grievance, a smaller gap or lower expectations to diminish it.[10] American ideology—the American dream—leads to the most ambitious and hopeful comparisons and so—with so large a gap in incomes and people *unable* to move up—the sense of grievance is great.

Exploring the disorders of the 1960s, the National Commission on the Causes and Prevention of violence saw relative deprivation as one of the major factors.[11] In these terms, one might expect social disorder not from the homeless and most deprived, who tend to have very low expectations, but from the working poor, the lower middle class, the students who strive for achievements they feel have been promised that always elude them.

More tuned to such issues than we are, in recent years European countries have absorbed talk of poverty into the broader term, "social exclusion." Anne Power, a professor at the London School of Economics, recently explained the term as follows:

Social exclusion is about the inability of our society to keep all groups and individuals within reach of what we expect as a society. It is about the tendency to push vulnerable and difficult individuals into the least popular places, furthest away from our common aspirations. It means that some people feel excluded from the mainstream, as though they do not belong.[12]

Thus, poverty is set within a context of inequality, segregation, ghettoization, stigma, and quarantine. And Power's term describes poverty—in some formal sense unplanned, but nonetheless created by "the system"—in the United States today.

Far-seeing de Tocqueville wrote that democracy is contingent on the tension between the competing forces of equality and freedom. Now equality, never robust, is at its lowest ebb in memory or in the statistical record—and still counting. This creates a problem for democracy and it contributes—in a communication-rich time, there can be little doubt about this—to the sense of grievance, of relative deprivation, of disaffection.

One does not predict disorder. We never seem to see it coming; moreover, a prediction may seem to verge on a threat or a call to disorder. But would it not be prudent to move back somewhat toward equality and so *prevent* difficulty?

ISSUES IN REFORMING WELFARE REFORM

What do we gather from our discussion so far about issues underlying how we might go about reforming welfare reform? Welfare is not a stand-alone program; except in a trivial sense, it cannot be corrected within its own confines. Welfare is another face of poverty wages and both are related to the distribution or maldistribution of income. The strategic question is, where is it most important that our society attack this constant companionship?

Improving low wages appears to be the key. As the history of welfare makes clear and current public opinion surveys confirm, welfare will not be improved in any way that makes it appear to be an attractive alternative to work, so wages come first. Moreover, higher wages have the advantage of contributing to fairer income distribution without necessarily requiring direct government spending or intervention, which is politically more difficult to do.

In any event, we have to confront our mad insistence that *every* adult (except those who are wealthy, retired, and so forth) work. If one partner in a two-parent family wants to stay home with a child, it is eminently desirable that he or she be able to do so. Wages for the working partner or wages with some government subsidy (welfare, food stamps, EITC, health insurance, tax credits, etc.) ought to be set at a level that makes this possible without risking poverty.

Single parents are a harder case. It is not in society's interest to pauperize such families—a large and growing segment of our population—in order to force these mothers (usually single-parent families are headed by mothers) into the labor force. If they have skills or education or, indeed, if they are not educated but can find work anyway, and they want to work, this should be encouraged and supported. If they cannot work or prefer to stay home with the children, however, the family should be assisted, through the preschool years at least, by some combination of support from the children's father and government programming.

We have seen that the official poverty level is unreasonably low. Virtually all the proposals for a new definition that have been offered would produce higher poverty levels than now, and they should. Experience teaches (see Chapter 9) that a figure approximating half of median income for a family of four—over $20,000 a year in 2000—is regarded by the general public as reasonable and reasonably possible to live on.

We have not raised the issue of education and do not propose to examine it, but offer this small comment. Obviously, a sound education is at the heart of capacity to earn a living, if not of simply being able to get along in the complicated world we have constructed. How to provide this would be the subject of another book—someone else's book—but it must seem obvious that a stable home, which can only be facilitated by decent provisions for income, would contribute to children being able to learn and grow into productive adults.

There are advantages for all of us in the society of fair shares and decent living standards for all which it lies within our power to construct—advantages for our health, for our welfare, for our security, and for the world in which our descendents will live.

NOTES

1. Katherine S. Newman. *No Shame in My Game: The Working Poor in the Inner City*. Knopf and Russell Sage: New York, 1999. Pp. 52–53.

2. John Rawls. *A Theory of Justice*. Cambridge: Harvard University Press, 1971. P. 62.

3. Isaac Shapiro and Robert Greenstein, "The Widening Income Gulf." Center on Budget and Policy Priorities, September 4, 1999. Figure 2. The estimates for 1999 are the last available from the Census Bureau.

4. Richard Harwood, "Is Class the Problem?" *International Herald Tribune*, July 23, 1997.

5. David Stout, "Odds Worsen in Hunt for Low-Income Rentals." *New York Times*, September 24, 1999. P. A14.

6. Human Development Report 1999. UN Development Program: Oxford University Press, 1999.

7. James Lardner, "A New Health Hazard: Economic Inequality." *The Washington Post National Weekly Edition*, August 24, 1998. P. 22.

8. Louis Uchitelle, "Even the Rich Can Suffer from Income Inequality." *New York Times*, November 15, 1998.

9. Harriet Orcutt Duleep, "Mortality and Income Inequality Among Economically Developed Countries." *Social Security Bulletin*, Summer 1995, v. 58, no. 2. P. 34.

10. W. G. Runciman, *Relative Deprivation and Social Justice*. Routledge & Kegan Paul: London, 1966.

11. Report of the National Advisory Commission on Civil Disorders. E. P. Dutton and Co.: New York, 1968.

12. Anne Power. *Poor Areas and Social Exclusion*. CASE paper 35, February 2000. Centre for Analysis of Social Exclusion: London School of Economics, London. P. 1.

Chapter Seven

Intimations of the
Dis-Welfare State: A Forecast

There is no limit to the imaginative practices that may spring up in this unprecedented society where third-world poverty cohabits with superpower wealth and so, although we begin with what is already known, as all forecasts do, we must then offer modest proposals of extrapolation.

If we continue on the path that we are pursuing to welfare reform, by the end of 2001 comparatively few families will remain on TANF. Very likely, states will exempt the maximum number of recipients that the law allows (20 percent) from the five-year- and-out requirement, so that the most severely handicapped families will continue on TANF for a time.

It was evident by 1999 that many families that leave TANF seek to return within a relatively short time. In Maryland, about 20 percent returned to the rolls after three months. In Cleveland, 26 percent of "successfully" closed cases, that is, cases closed because a parent was working, returned to TANF within six months; in Wisconsin about 30 percent returned after fifteen months. As the deadline approaches, however, states will bob and weave to avoid restoring people to TANF.

That is, states will have special programs that provide large grants for car repairs so people can get to work or to buy clothing so they can dress acceptably for work. States will make heroic efforts to expand daycare, but its quality will not improve and may in fact deteriorate. They will create grants to subsidize the cost of housing for people leaving TANF. And they will invest heavily in energizing outreach to see that entitled people sign up for food stamps and Medicaid. Here and there, people with common sense may ask why states don't simply give needy people the money being spent on subsidies and social and health services, but states will resist this idea. Too much has been invested professionally and emotionally in e.w.a.w.k.i.

Adults in many families that once received assistance will be working, the majority of them in "contingent" jobs, temporary or part-time, generally without health insurance or other benefits, and many of them at odd hours. A minority, perhaps one out of five, will have family income that exceeds the poverty level. Still, many will not be working and it will not be clear how they are managing.

Indeed, a great deal will not be known. Although many will receive food stamps or commodities from hunger centers, these are not in themselves enough for adequate nutrition, so the extent of malnutrition will not be clear and it will not be clear how they meet other needs, if at all. As with people who left TANF earlier, a third (probably more by 2001) will, when asked, complain of missed meals and many will say that they cannot pay their rent or meet their bills.

How family arrangements were affected will be murky; how children are making out will not be known in any reliable way. Researching these issues is difficult and relatively little will have been done or done properly. Recipients who were dropped from TANF will merge into the working poor; others will disappear entirely, the first *desaparecidos* (disappeared ones) of the third millennium.

The working poor will number 20 million, perhaps more (in addition to poor families without a working member, of course).

One may hazard the guess that many children who were former recipients and many children who would have been new recipients will have been moved about in ways that were noted in Chapter 4—to relatives, to friends and neighbors, to foster homes, and then around again. Many will live in households where they or their mothers are subject to abuse.

A sizeable number of children will be in foster care and many will have been offered for adoption. Prospective adoptive parents will no longer have to travel to China or Russia as they do now—no further than to the inner city—to see a healthy child of a desirable ethnicity, even an infant, who is available for adoption. Entrepreneurs will set up websites to connect children and adoptive parents. There will not be enough acceptable adoptive or foster family homes for all the children who need care and children's institutions will be established or expanded to accommodate them. We have long experience with children's institutions: in the long run, they work out badly. Yet, that is the way we will go.

In time, the need of parents, desperate for food and shelter for their children and themselves, may find a fit with the need for domestic help of struggling middle-class parents, pressed to arrange care for their own children and have their homes attended to while they work. So poor families may indenture themselves to middle-class families for a period of time while the children grow up—for 10 years, say—in exchange for guaranteed food, shelter, and schooling, but no wages to speak of.

In addition to child care and household service, opportunities might include serving as surrogate mothers; fertilization would be arranged, one way or another. For historical reasons, black people will avoid indentured servitude, if at all possible.

The U.S. Immigration and Naturalization Service (INS) has estimated that upwards of 55,000 foreigners a year enter the United States illegally and work as indentured servants. Generally speaking, INS does not have the resources to search out and prosecute these families. Those whom it finds are deported for illegal entry but their employers are not prosecuted. It would not be a great departure for U.S. citizens to usurp the role that illegal aliens now assume.

Evaluations will show that almost 100 percent of those who have indentured themselves are working, indeed, working very hard; with zero cost to the government, that is, with infinite cost-effectiveness. Some will wonder why the practice was not thought of long ago (but it was, of course). As usual, central issues about how children and families are managing will provide difficult to research and so, relying largely on statistics of how many are working and are not receiving welfare, indenture will be judged to be successful.

New areas of labor law and civil rights law will be opened up. Does the U.S. Department of Labor have the responsibility or right to inspect working conditions with respect to indentured servants? Do child labor and minimum wage laws apply in what is essentially a family matter? Civil rights challenges may be raised, arguing that involuntary servitude is unconstitutional; the counterargument will be offered that this servitude is voluntary and the contracts are valid. Still, there will be pressure to amend the constitution.

In a not entirely unrelated development, in the last few years model prison labor programs, previously devoted to making license plates and furniture for government offices, have expanded into substantial commercial enterprises. Prisoners now do everything from telemarketing to assembling computer circuit boards. In 2000, there were 80,000 such prison jobs, many for private employers and paying as much as $7.00 an hour, plus free room and board. With a record high of more than two million prisoners in the country, there is plenty of room to expand these work programs.

Proponents cite studies that show that prisoners who work in such jobs are less likely to commit crimes when they are released. The practice is profitable for state governments and for private industry as well, of course, so there will be much support for such programs. These penal public employment programs will not pass unremarked by people who, for one reasons and another, cannot find jobs at all, who may, in 2004 or 2006, volunteer to be imprisoned and inquire whether they must first commit a crime. Progressive prisons will experiment with family incarceration plans.

The poor—working and not working—will include heavy representations of minorities, women, young adults, and other disadvantaged groups. A gaping schism in our society will widen and deepen, made graphic by the fact that so many of the "underclass," as they will surely be called, are segregated in contractual or walled institutions. The upper classes will have their own walls—secure buildings, gated communities, and island havens.

Tensions among the underclass, the middle classes, and the truly wealthy will be aggravated. All classes will feel increasing anxiety about crime and immorality, even though these may not have increased. The language of class conflict will be inflamed, with much talk about underclass, genetic tendencies, criminality, and their rhetorical equivalents. The poorer classes will find a language of their own for their situation.

THE STATES' PROBLEM

We have noted that the states have received a windfall because federal payments for TANF were based on the years before the steep TANF-precipitated decline in caseload. Out of $34.4 billion given to states between 1997 and 1999, only $27 billion was actually spent, according to a *New York Times* analysis.[1] See Appendix A, Table A-2.

States varied in their behavior about the surpluses in their treasuries. For example, Wisconsin raised its benefit levels by 20 percent and provided an array of new benefits that would support beneficiaries' efforts to work. On the other hand, Idaho, Ohio, and Wyoming saved their money. At work in these variations are judgments whether to help as much as resources will allow, to save the money for a time when it will be needed, or to use it for other purposes.

According to the Center on Budget and Policy Priorities in Washington, D.C., a number of states used TANF funds to replace money already allocated for social services—$48 million in Connecticut, $100 million in Minnesota, $162 million in Texas, $120 mil-

lion in Michigan.[2] *The New York Times* reported that New York's
Governor George Pataki acknowledged that $1 billion had been
used for tax cuts and other state budgetary priorities.[3]

When the five-year time limit descends at the end of 2001, states
will find that while their allocations of state funds for these purposes have been lowered, the most difficult cases remain on their
welfare roles. These are women without a high school education,
many of them addicted to drugs, some of them physically or mentally ill, some taking care of handicapped children for whom there
is no alternative care. According to the law, states may exempt as
much as 20 percent of the welfare caseload from work requirements, but New York State, for example, estimates that it may be
left with 40 percent of its caseload still active.

Presumably, Congress will relent and provide some financing
for the excess caseload but, chances are, it will not be generous.
That states used TANF money for unrelated purposes will not
draw sympathy. Moreover, Congress gave the states a windfall
with the original funding formula for TANF. In exchange, the legislation freed Congress from meeting the open-ended costs of AFDC.
Not much attention was paid to this Faustian bargain that states accepted—indeed, lobbied for—at the time, but Congress was well
aware of what it was doing. In 2001, then, the states will face the
prospect of a huge financial burden for which it has no committed
or reserve funds.

WILL THE PUBLIC REACT?

Will there be a public outcry against such desperate poverty as
has been described, against so many homeless people on the
streets, against so many children reported as abused and ne-
glected, against the surge of children into the care of public agencies? Will we recognize that the sense of community that it is said so
many of us avidly seek is being destroyed by our own policies?
Some believe that such a reaction is the only hope for reversal of
dis-welfare policies[4] and that there *will* be an outcry, but there are
reasons to be dubious about this, as follows.

People who are old enough remember the time when homeless people were few and homeless families with children on the streets virtually unknown. The notion that we would tolerate family homelessness would have seemed fanciful. Yet we *have* tolerated it for some years. The idea that we would tolerate having 42 million people without coverage for medical care would have seemed fanciful. Yet, widespread discontent with our system of medical care does not focus on these uncovered people but rather on the difficulties encountered by those who do have coverage.

Why don't citizens besiege congressional offices on behalf of the most needy? Answers to this question tend to deal with the postmodern prevalence of greed—the me-first phenomenon in American society; this must certainly be a factor. The growing alienation of Americans from our government, of which the steady decline in voting is prime evidence; this is also a factor. A feeling of powerlessness with respect to government and the corporate economy must account for the failure of aggrieved groups themselves—for example, struggling moderate-income families, those *with* health-care insurance who are treated badly by their HMOs, or the homeless—to organize effectively on their own behalf.

These phenomena—greed and feelings of alienation and powerlessness—are not new, of course, but they appear to have deepened in the last decades.

Another factor is the confusion of messages. It does not help that there are studies that may be said to support any point of view. Nor does it help that the most effective communicators are, after all, those with the most money, who do not necessarily pursue the general welfare. Their power with respect to these policies tends to be hidden behind "the decorous drapery of political democracy," in the words of R. H. Tawney.[5]

Still another factor is the failure to grasp the connection between the immediate, visible program and the broad or remote policy that is responsible for it. Apart from a few hardliners, for example, nobody really wants to see homelessness. However, a genuine solution reaches into the economics of housing: interest rates on mortgages, banking industry practices, the government's willingness to subsidize moderate-income housing, and so forth. Such problems involve, at their roots, extensive special interests that are generally averse to change. The public does not grasp what these interests are or the self-interest (of banking and other financial interests in this case) that drives their opposition to long-term solutions. Serious reform is paralyzed by this disconnectedness; instead, we develop handicraft devices (shelters for the homeless, outreach programs for Medicaid) that are better than nothing, but are not solutions.

All this will have to be worked out in the face of state budget crises that pit needy people against tax cuts or the needs of public education, for example. A powerful public reaction against the construction of the dis-welfare state is not a foregone conclusion. Michael Sandel, a Harvard University professor of government, has offered the following comment:

Today's accumulation of enormous wealth is unparalleled since the last Gilded Age. But the Gilded Age of a century ago brought in its wake a wave of progressive reform and public investment—in parks, libraries, schools, and municipal projects. Today's Gilded Age, by contrast, hasn't generated any comparable resolve to ease the effects of inequality by strengthening public institutions.[6]

One must offer two caveats about the forecasts that have been offered here. First, we usually do not know when social movements are imminent and the various grassroots groups—environmentalists, health-care activists, living wage organizers—may come together to move a different agenda, as happened after the last Gilded Age.

Second, if and when we have a long-deferred recession, all bets will be off. The misery of former TANF recipients, whose income, inadequate to begin with, will plummet, may not impress very many other people, but job losses and deflation will realize the worst nightmares of the middle classes. Their distress and resentment would be politically significant. Obviously, the two possible developments are related: a recession could ignite a nascent social movement for reform.

Reform takes shape around programs. The next two chapters outline the direction that reform, when and if it comes, ought to take.

NOTES

1. Jason DeParle, "Leftover Money for Welfare Baffles, or Inspires, States," *New York Times*, August 29, 1999. P. 1.

2. Edward Lazere, "Welfare Balances after Three Years of Block Grants." Center on Budget and Policy Priorities: Washington, D.C., January 2000.

3. Raymond Hernandez, "Federal Welfare Windfall Frees New York Money for Other Uses." *New York Times*, April 23, 2000. P. 1.

4. Government policies that cause positive damage to citizens, especially to poor and disadvantaged citizens, are dis-welfare policies, in the usage of the late Richard M. Titmuss, professor and policy expert at the London School of Economics—a truly civilized man, whose broad influence is missed. See D.A. Reisman, *Richard Titmuss—Welfare and Society*. Heinemann: London, 1977. Preface by R.A. Pinker. P. x.

5. R.H. Tawney, "The Choice before the Labour Party," *The Attack* (London). 1953.

6. Quoted in James Fallows, "The Invisible Poor." *Sunday New York Times Magazine*, March 19, 2000. P. 112.

Chapter Eight

Seven Guides

Implicit in everything that has been said here is the message that the problems of welfare reform are not fundamentally technical; they do not primarily concern program design. Rather, they reflect deep, longstanding divisions in American society.

Welfare, as we knew it and as we know it, is the woodshed in which we heap up people who embody our prejudices—against minorities,[1] against women, against children. We may not define our own attitudes as prejudices, but these prejudices operate most frankly in connection with poor people, because our deepest fear and contempt arise from class differences. For each of us, clicking on poverty lights up every latent prejudice.

Notwithstanding protestations of sympathy and helpfulness, welfare reform was a product of long-smoldering public suspicion and resentment. Its design and administration reflect this. TANF recipients were launched and continue to be launched into a soci-

ety in which they are ill prepared to function and which is not prepared to accept and support them.

They do not have the background or skills that will secure jobs
that pay enough to live on. Conversely, the market does not provide enough decent jobs for them and pay scales are not adequate.
These are not isolated disparities that can be corrected on a broad
scale by a collective bargaining agreement or the stroke of a pen on
one legislative bill. They are inextricable from economic issues
about profits and the distribution of income, which powerfully impede improvement.

And they cannot be adjusted without affecting other groups of
people, the working poor or marginally non-poor, for example. We
have undertaken to clear out the woodshed, but the house and gar-
den are not prepared.

None of this denies the strides that have been made in the last 40
years in race and gender relations—occupational, educational, and
political gains, desegregation of some suburban housing and the
visible appearance of blacks, hispanics, and women in athletics,
entertainment, and government and executive suites. Nor does it
deny the millions of hours that Americans devote to volunteer activities and to day-to-day neighborliness.

But most poor people are beyond the reach of simple, direct
charity and we do not see them. This is not entirely because they
and we live separately, as of course we do, but because *we do not see
them*. We watch them pay with food stamps in the supermarket or
we walk past them where they lie on the street, and we do not see
them. We say that they are invisible but it is irritation that blinds us.
Therefore, we do not make the *collective* provisions that would
greatly ameliorate poverty. We have lost our grasp of the turmoil
and fellow feeling that produced the Social Security Act, the Civil
Rights Act of 1964, the G.I. Bill of Rights.

Facing this view of our society, one is tempted to call first of all
for an awakening, a new consciousness, a moral regeneration, but
it appears that we do not have prophets who can command attention. If a Joseph arose among us to admonish us to share our grain,
would we know him? Such calls, for we have such calls, eloquently,

urgently, are filed away with donations to United Way and thoughts for the Sabbath. We are well defended, as psychotherapists say.

Here, we have not launched directly into the programs that would chart a radically different course from the 1996 welfare reform because I do not want to represent that the main issue is programmatic. The main issue is how we feel about one another, how we feel about all of us as one people. Unless there is some sense of brotherhood or fraternity—sisterhood or sorority would do as well—program proposals are idle. This is the point: It has to be clear that we have lost our way as a society. The 1996 welfare reform is merely one evidence of that. Offering program proposals does not imply that the proposals, in themselves, are the main point or that they may be readily enacted.

GUIDES FOR PROGRAM CHOICES

It is perhaps a minority view that we make social progress by inventing institutions that we then clothe with attitudes. Thus, social security was not an expression of the practice of retirement; rather, the practice of retirement grew up around the institution of social security. The institution created the practice; the attitudes followed. Similarly, despite all its difficulties, national health insurance in Canada and in the countries of Europe binds the people of each of these countries together. It is as rabbis have been heard to say to nonbelievers: "Practice the rituals and you will come to believe."

The program proposals in the next chapter create or improve institutions that reflect a feeling of national community and would foster such a feeling. Before turning to them, we set out here some of the principles that should guide program choices.

The following six principles are garnered from earlier chapters.

1. A broad-scale program must have, or be able to achieve, a level of common public acceptance in order to work well for a long time (Chapter 3).
2. It must be administered by units that accept its basic objectives (Chapter 3).

3. Its operations must achieve some level of funding adequacy (Chapter 3).

4. It is futile for it to set objectives that everything around it frustrates, as if ghetto hospital administrators thought themselves principally responsible for maintaining a healthy population (Chapter 3).

5. Social norms and the programs related to them should support a wage for full-time work that would sustain a family of three with at least minimum adequacy (Chapters 4, 5, and 6).

6. A single parent or one parent in a family with two adults should have sufficient income to stay at home and refrain from outside work—if they choose to—during the time that they have preschool children (Chapters 5 and 6). Obviously, this principle depends in large measure on principle 5, above.

One more principle: 7. The Means Test. A means-tested program is one that conditions eligibility on an individual demonstration of need, that is, on proof that income or assets are not adequate for the needs of a person or family. Obviously, need must be defined for the purposes of each program.

Welfare, food stamps, and Medicaid are means-tested programs. Social security, unemployment insurance, and Medicare do not require a demonstration of need; they are not means tested. If one thinks about it, the eligibility conditions that *are* required for these latter programs—old age, unemployment, being handicapped, widowed, or orphaned—are surrogates for need (imperfect surrogates, to be sure). Hence, it turns out that these non-means-tested programs are important in avoiding or relieving poverty. Still, the difference makes a difference: every beneficiary of either type of program feels the difference, one way or the other.

In practice in the United States, means-tested programs turn out very badly; welfare is a prime example. They carry a sense of social stigma, so that many people are reluctant to apply for benefits and those who do apply often feel humiliated. For example, we have noted the frustrating shortfall in enrollment for food stamps and Medicaid (see Chapter 4). Considerable efforts launched to enroll those who do not apply, even though eligible, have met with indifferent success.

Even SSI, a relatively uncontroversial means-tested program for the elderly and disabled, administered by the Social Security Administration, enrolls only about half of those who are eligible, "possibly because of the stigma associated with receiving need-based . . . payments," a study by Richard W. Johnson for the Urban Institute observes.[2]

This is not a new problem. In a recent history of social welfare, Linda Gordon describes an address by Frank Bruno during the depths of the depression in the 1930s. He

redefined pauperization in the service of social reform: No longer were paupers created primarily by too-easy handouts, the older social work anxiety. Rather, "It was the experience of defeat, the emotional frustration, the unrewarded effort . . . to gain a foothold upon the slippery industrial banks, which finally broke their spirit. . . . And as if that were not enough, we have erected . . . a condition of eligibility for relief which still further convinces them that struggle is useless."[3]

Stigma in means-tested programs is not a one-way street. The shame of applicants is met with the blame or suspicion of officials (see Chapter 4). A striking illustration of this is the record of the Internal Revenue Service (IRS). In 1999, it was more likely to audit poor than rich people—one of 74 taxpayers with income under $25,000 but only one of 87 whose income was above $100,000.

There were many accusations of fraud in applying for EITC, but the amount of money that might be recovered from the poor was insignificant compared to what audits regularly recovered from the rich. It made no sense; only the vulnerability of the poor and the fact that Congress and the IRS were more profoundly suspicious of them than of the rich could explain this phenomenon.

Means testing has other problems. The level of expenditure and the quality of administration of government programs are not fixed by initial legislation but are a continuous function of the interest and power of the programs' constituencies. The constituency of means-tested programs comprises, by definition, the most powerless people in the country. Therefore, the promise to do well with means-tested programs, whatever the immediate national impulse, is, in the long run, never carried out.

Common sense may seem to suggest that means testing is good for poor people because the money intended for them goes to them with very little waste, but it does not work out like that. With a growing economy, payment levels in means-tested programs grow very little and even lose ground, while other transfer programs flourish. For example, in 1970, the average monthly payment for an AFDC family was $183, and in 1996, $386; it had doubled over the course of 26 years. But monthly payments for orphaned and dependent children under social security increased from $37 to $188, a five-fold increase (neither pair of figures is corrected for inflation).

Perhaps one should examine the issue of means testing across countries. Walter Korpi and Joakim Palme have studied a dozen industrial countries, publishing their findings in the *American Sociological Review*. "The more we target benefits at the poor [that is, use means-testing]," they write, "the *less likely* we are to reduce poverty and inequality" (emphasis added).[4] Poor people get a large share of the means-tested benefits allocated to them but, assigned to receive their benefits from a means-tested program, they lose far more in other transfer payments.

Thus, a seventh principle by which to govern policy is to use other mechanisms for assisting poor people and to rely relatively little on means testing. To be sure, some means-tested programs will always be needed. It is not reasonable to expect to design programs that deal with every contingency, but the question is one of balance.

NOTES

1. For an exploration of the reach of racism into current welfare practices see Martin Gilens, *Why Americans Hate Welfare: Race, Media and the Politics of Antipoverty Policy*. University of Chicago Press 1999. See also Matthew Diller, "The Revolution in Welfare Administration." *NYU Law Review*, 75 no. 5, November 2000. PP. 1121–1220.

2. Richard W. Johnson, "The Redistributional Implications of Reductions in Social Security COLAs," The Retirement Project,

Brief Series no. 5, June, 1999. Urban Institute: Washington, D.C. P. 3.

   3. Linda Gordon. *Pitied But Not Entitled: Single Mothers and the History of Welfare*, Free Press, 1994. P. 221. Frank J. Bruno was Dean of the School of Social Work at Washington University in St. Louis—a prominent social worker in a hard time. Citing him is an act of homage; he was my teacher.

   4. Walter Korpi and Joakim Palme, "The Paradox of Redistribution and Strategies of Equality: Welfare State Institutions, Inequality, and Poverty in Western Countries." *American Sociological Review*, v. 63, October 1998. P. 661.

Chapter Nine

The Lady, or the Tiger?

Setting a different course for welfare reform, that is, greatly reducing poverty in the country, requires that we improve low-end and moderate wage levels and seek fairer income shares. It is a stunningly difficult and complex undertaking. In the material that follows, we deal mainly with wages, income maintenance policies such as EITC, and health care. Our approach to these may provide an indication of how other systems would be dealt with as well.

Wages are the single most important element of policy with respect to welfare, poverty, and fair shares. Income maintenance policies are also of commanding importance.

WAGE LEVELS

Aiming at the lowest income that a family of four may reasonably be expected to live on—$20,000, according to public opinion polls—a full-time worker must earn at least $10 an hour. As it happens, this figure accords roughly with the view of economists such as Victor Fuchs, Harold Watts, and Timothy Smeeding, who have relied (in 1967, 1980, and 1999, respectively) on a poverty level representing half of median family income or expenditures from year to year.[1] If one assumes that the median family income in the coming years will exceed $40,000, then (at current prices) $20,000 a year or $10 an hour for full-time, year-round work is the very least that will be required for a decent standard of living.

We are not now discussing the minimum wage—$10 an hour is a far cry from $5.15 or the enhancement that Congress has considered—$6.15. (A higher minimum wage is eminently desirable on its own merits, of course.) Ten dollars an hour is a low-end wage that generally would be regarded as reasonable. Even if there is not a second worker or other supplementary income, a family might be expected to manage to live on it. At year 2000 prices, $10 begins to be a *family wage*; as such, it might widely be seen as respectable by the public and so, in the end, by employers.

The attempt to arrive at wages and salaries upward from $10 an hour would arouse scornful cries from right-leaning economists and the business interests that invoke their support. In time-honored fashion, they will predict loss of jobs, small businesses going bankrupt, and inflation out of control; all *failed* predictions that are offered each time raising the minimum wage is at issue.

We must leave these arguments to the economists. We note only that such arguments lose most of their force if rising wages are not dutifully paid for by consumers but impel a return to the relationship not so many years ago between wages, on one hand, and profits or the return on capital, on the other. Or, rising wages might impel greater management efficiency. In any event, the objective must be approached by increments; the difficult question here is how.

Over the last quarter of a century, wages have become increasingly unequal. Wages have behaved as if they were tied to academic achievement, falling in that period for those with less than a full four-year college degree and falling most of all for those who went no further than high school. Only people with college degrees are earning more than their predecessors—three times as much as those who have not completed high school.

A dozen distinguishable reasons are offered for this splitting of the labor market. Two prominent economists, Richard B. Freeman and Lawrence F. Katz, have attempted to quantify the contribution of various factors to wage inequality during the 1980s. According to their analysis, the most powerful contributing factors were, first, the shift from a goods-producing to a service economy; second, freer trade and immigration; third, declining union membership; and fourth, an acceleration of new technology, especially a shift to new information technologies.[2]

Scholars dispute this ranking and it is the stuff of heated political dispute, about trade and immigration policy, in particular. Of the four, however, the factor most amenable to public influence would appear to be trade union membership. We focus here on the public climate surrounding union organization, collective bargaining, and government regulation of these activities. A brief review of how we arrived at the climate today may help in framing recommendations.

Labor Organization and Collective Bargaining

It may be difficult to recall or accept that public opinion once supported trade union organization and at least rough equity in collective bargaining, but it did. The National Labor Relations Act of 1935 was enacted out of workers' rebellion against oppressive treatment and poor pay levels and was supported by citizen revulsion at widespread corporate abuse of its disproportionate power relative to unions.

The Wagner Act, named for its prime sponsor Senator Robert F. Wagner, greatly strengthened labor unions' capacity to organize and to conduct collective bargaining. Union strength grew from 12 percent of the nonfarm labor force in 1933 to 32 percent in 1947, a membership level that was sustained into the late 1950s. Many other forces contributed to this growth. As one example, unions had grown particularly strong in industries like steel and construction that burgeoned during our conduct of World War II; union membership grew as those work forces expanded.

Under governmental and public pressure, there developed what older labor union people now nostalgically refer to as a "social contract" and what academic observers spoke of as an "accord"—an unwritten code of civilized conduct between corporations and unions. If a union won a representation election, the employer would promptly begin to bargain with the union, seeking to arrive at a mutually acceptable agreement. If a union struck a plant, when the strike was over the people who had left would resume their jobs. Much of this was overseen by the National Labor Relations Board (NLRB), which reflected public views and tended to be sympathetic to unions.

Sympathy began to dissipate shortly after the war ended, with charges of concentration of power in top union echelons and undue, even reckless, use of union power. The change in climate produced the Labor-Management Relations Act of 1947, called the Taft-Hartley Act after its congressional sponsors. Among provisions designed to weaken unions in relation to employers was one permitting states to outlaw the "closed shop" (union contracts requiring all employees to belong to the union); another outlawed "secondary boycotts" (union pressure on a business not directly involved in a labor dispute to keep it from doing business with an employer that *is* directly involved); and one provision expanded the NLRB from three to five members, permitting the immediate addition of two members who would be sympathetic to employers.

In the succeeding half-century, labor unions have suffered a series of disabling blows, not all legislative, by any means, that undermined their capacity to organize or to bargain to a successful conclusion. For example, the Landrum-Griffin Act of 1959 tightened the Taft-Hartley Act, adding new restrictions on strikes, picketing, and boycotts, And revelations about corruption and close relations with organized crime damaged unions' public image.

Corporations understood quite well that deep hostility between management and workers had helped to create the Wagner Act. In response, they undertook to professionalize plant personnel management and to manage their plants more democratically, initiating recreation programs for workers and corporate-involvement programs such as "quality circles." As employee–management partnerships flourished and with job tenure fostered by a generally stable economy, businesses gained lifetime loyalty from many employees.

Further, drawing on consultants with sophisticated strategies for dealing with unions, businesses learned how to resist organizing drives without resorting to the police or the National Guard. Barely noticed at first, the "social contract" or "accord" evaporated. This change was dramatically marked when airline traffic controllers went out on strike in 1981 and President Ronald Reagan, newly in office, announced that they would not be rehired. Even at some apparent risk to the flying public until new traffic controllers could be properly trained, the government held to this position. Around the country, unions and businessmen and - women took note.

For such reasons—restrictive legislation, an increasingly unfriendly NLRB and government, a poor union image, an improved workplace environment, steadily rising wages over two decades, media- and strategy-conscious management, not to mention more far-reaching changes like the migration of jobs from organized heavy industries to the unorganized service sector—union membership dropped over the years, from about one-third of the labor force in the 1950s to 13 or 14 percent currently. Declining membership itself added to difficulty in organizing unorganized workers.

This cursory review omits a great deal that is important and is intended only to say that the economic power of employers and workers relative to each other cycles and responds to citizen perceptions of equity. This relationship is now greatly overweighted on the side of employers. More than half a century after the Taft-Hartley Act, the time has come for a correction and one may glimpse signs that a correction may be attainable.

Such attachment as businesses once had to the communities in which plants are located is declining as a result of corporate mergers, not to mention globalization. With rapid obsolescence of job skills and with large-scale layoffs of personnel (what Alan Greenspan once opaquely called "the heightened level of potential job dismissal") the norm, few workers expect to be able to assert a right to retain a job, no matter how long they have held it. Therefore, the lifetime loyalty that employers once fostered and were able to attain is disappearing.

The labor-management "social contract" is fading into history. As the Department of Labor counts employment, in the year 2000 we have very little unemployment. One might therefore expect a satisfied workforce; yet, as surveys testify, workers are widely uneasy, in large measure because they feel that their jobs are insecure—and how would they not feel insecure? The steady growth in real income of low-paid, moderately-paid, and even middle-income workers has long since faded away. And workers are well aware that, while they struggle to meet their expenses, a portion of the population lives very well indeed. Thus, some of the factors that have represented a brake on the capacity of unions to organize are reversing.

In recent years, organized labor launched a major recruiting drive, which had some, but far from spectacular, success. This is in part, no doubt, because the same insecurity that makes workers uneasy makes them fearful of drawing management attention. It is also because government regulation is now so largely stacked against the unions. It is, therefore, particularly important that citizens grasp the role of trade unions in balancing the power of businesses and the right of workers to seek what they regard as a decent wage. Beyond this, the basic legislation and the regulations governing this relationship need now to be adjusted to facilitate a correction.

Movement toward correction and an acceptable low-end wage should include such steps as these:

- Spread the practice adopted by a number of cities around the country of contracting only with employers that undertake to pay at least a "living wage," commonly $9 or $10 an hour.

- Increase penalties on employers that illegally dismiss workers who try to organize a union.

- Provide oversight to assure that employers bargain in good faith when a union has won an election. As an example of situations that should be avoided, the Teamsters Union embarked on a six-month-long strike against the Overnite Transportation Company when managers refused to negotiate seriously after the union had won an election to represent the company's workers.

- Ban permanent replacement of striking workers, as in the strike of air traffic controllers mentioned earlier.

- Assure union representatives access to workers at the workplace that is equal to the access of management.

- Clear away the bureaucratic maze and other impediments that keep the NLRB from acting promptly on its workload.

In the latter half of the 20th century, the labor movement learned a painful lesson that one of its leaders, Samuel Gompers, taught in the 19th century that what the government gives it can take away. Labor unions need government help now but, in the end, they will have to rely on their own struggle to attain rough equity. And in the end, the nation will not have low-end $10 an hour wages from policy statements but only from the determination of workers to assure it, as some are attempting to do.

INCOME MAINTENANCE POLICIES

As so many families will have income from work that is well below the $20,000 a year figure that seems to be a reasonable minimum, and as so many families will have no income from work at all, even in these prosperous times, the nation needs programs that provides at least some cash to these families, particularly to families that include children. The program that is most prominent now is the EITC, described at the end of Chapter 2.

The Earned Income Tax Credit

The EITC now costs about $30 billion a year, more than was spent on AFDC. Although targeted at poor people, as AFDC was and TANF is, the tax credit is only available to a person who has income from work; indeed, in order to encourage work, the EITC payment increases as income from work increases, up to a point.

For example, a family with two children who have $9,500 in income from work would, upon filing a proper tax return, have a $3,800 EITC payment in addition. As income from work increases, however, the family loses $1 in EITC for every $5 of earnings over $12,500. Is this fair? Well, there did not appear to be much point in paying $3,800 to families with incomes of $40,000 or $50,000 or more.

The EITC is an important program, moving almost five million people over the poverty line in 1999. As we face the virtual end of welfare, it is just as well that this income tax credit is in place, but it has been criticized on a variety of grounds.

It has been accused of undermining incentive to work, but it is not as if $9,500 + $3,800, the maximum EITC allowance, provides a comfortable resting place for a family with two children. Such evidence as there is suggests that, if anything, the EITC somewhat increases the tendency to work, presumably because it makes it seem possible to get by on low wages instead of resorting to strategies other than work.

It is also criticized for being extensively subject to fraud, but examination suggests that much of what is called fraud is confusion that arises out of a maze of intricate rules and regulations. In any event, EITC abuse, if that is what it is, is not more frequent than the rate of abuse in higher-income tax returns, and costs the government far less.

Finally, the EITC is, in principle, a means-tested program and so is flawed in the ways that all means-tested programs are likely to be (see Chapter 8). However, it is so far not administered in the peculiarly mean, case-by-case fashion that AFDC was and TANF is. Given the social climate of the United States and, for that matter, the industrial world in the year 2000, it does not appear that any reasonable, non-means-tested alternative could be enacted. Therefore, the EITC is badly needed and, as it does have defects, it ought to be refashioned and improved.

How Might the EITC Be Improved?

The EITC ought to be simplified; this much is clear. The benefit (a maximum of $3,800 for a family with two children) starts to decline when a family earns more than $12,500, leaving most families well short of $20,000. Either the maximum benefit ought to be increased, or the point at which the benefit starts to decline ought to be raised, or both. And finally, benefits are currently not increased for families with three or more children; there should be an increment for each child.

In 1999, eleven states (Colorado, Iowa, Kansas, Maryland, Massachusetts, Minnesota, New York, Oregon, Rhode Island, Vermont, and Wisconsin) enhanced the federal EITC with small credits of their own. By and large, these states simply added a percentage of the federal EITC, which they paid to families. The add-on varied considerably (by state, by number of children, and by income), from 4 to 50 percent of the federal level. Obviously, benefits can be made more generous in at least some of these states and states that do not have add-ons should introduce them.

Instead of improving each benefit, one may think of combining the EITC with other child benefits in the income tax system. In particular, the income tax exemption for dependents—$2,750 for each dependent in 1999—has the perverse effect of being worth more to higher-income families. For example, a family with income so low that it is not liable for income tax gains nothing at all from the exemption; the exemption is not "refundable." A low-income family gains 15 percent of $2,750. However, higher-income taxpayers are ahead by up to 40 percent of $2,750.

Two economists, Robert Cherry at Brooklyn College and Max B. Sawicky at the Economic Policy Institute, a Washington, D.C., think tank, have proposed combining three existing programs into a single program called the Universal Unified Child Credit (UUCC).[3] The three programs are the EITC, the income tax exemption for children, and the "child tax credit" ($500 per child). At a cost of $32 billion a year, the UUCC would simplify application for benefits and would enhance benefit levels for low-income people.

At 1999 rates, families with taxable income at or below $43,000 a year would come out ahead.

A serious limitation of the EITC, and of the UUCC proposals just described, is that they make no provision for families who have and are likely to have little or no income from work. Broadly speaking, these are single mothers with young children; mothers who are mentally or physically ill but capable of caring for their children, or whose children, are handicapped (but do not qualify for SSI). They are mothers in locations or at moments in our society when there are not jobs for them, of which there are more than a few. They are mothers who have no way to get to where the jobs are, a serious problem in many large cities and rural areas. They are families for which adequate daycare is not available.

In short, they are people whom TANF discovers in numerous cases but to whose stark need states are blind as a matter of policy. It is unconscionable that there should be no national provision for them at all. Where there are young children, a reasonable social policy would make it possible for single parents or for one of two parents, including those not characterized by the difficulties listed above, to stay at home (see chapter 5).

A step toward dealing with this inequity would be to double the child tax credit, now $500 per child, to $1,000 for each child under six years of age and make it refundable.[4] That is, most families would receive a credit against their tax and families that do not owe that amount would receive a check from the government. This would add very modestly to the income of all families, including young families that are without work or have very low-paid jobs.

Most of its cost would be met by wiping out the current income tax exemption for children under six years of age. All families would get the same benefit for their young children in place of the current disproportionate benefit for those with higher incomes. The highest income families would wind up with a derisory net increase in taxes.

SPECIAL PROBLEMS

Out-Sourcing

It has increasingly become the practice for employers to contract out work to legitimate independent contractors. Using part-time or temporary employees, contractors produce parts, handle complete operations for businesses, or furnish them with temporary assistance. Among a variety of advantages that the practice offers, contractors are legally able to minimize tax payments for Unemployment Insurance and Worker's Compensation and, typically, they provide little or no health or other benefits; the savings may be shared with the employer.

Thus the workers, who are relatively low-paid in the first place, find that they are not covered when they suffer unemployment or injury on the job or become ill. In a 1998 study for the Urban Institute, policy analyst Wayne Vroman concluded that the unemployment rate for former welfare recipients is twice as high as the rate for all unemployed persons. Yet, no more than 20 percent of the former recipients are eligible for unemployment benefits—compared to 60 to 70 percent of all unemployed persons.[5]

The remedy seems obvious: tighten the requirement for contributions to social insurance funds for part-time and temporary employees.

Health Care

Securing health care is a considerable problem for low-income Americans. A major reason is that coverage by employers, which accounts for 90 percent of all private health-care coverage, has been declining dramatically. The number of uncovered people rises steadily, to 42.6 million at last count. A Commonwealth Fund survey in 1999 found that 40 percent of working-age adults with incomes under $20,000 did not have health insurance. Among these 40 percent who were working, 40 percent of *them* were uncovered because they did not have employer-sponsored plans available to them or they could not afford to pay their share of premiums.

Under-insurance is an additional problem. More than half of the more than one million Americans who filed for bankruptcy last year did so, at least in part, because they could not deal with medical bills.[6] For middle-class families, under-insurance was more common than no insurance at all and produced bankruptcies.

It is difficult to frame a solution for these problems. The overwhelming tendency these days is to extend the reach of Medicaid and other means-tested programs. However, moderate- and middle-income people would not qualify for means-tested programs. And inbred institutional practices impede the delivery of means-tested health care to low-income people who, for their part, resist signing up anyway (see Chapter 4).

Moreover, states resist expanding programs that require them to pay a share of the cost, as Medicaid does. For example, when Congress enacted TANF in 1996, it set aside $500 million to assure that families would not lose Medicaid when they lost cash assistance. Almost four years later, despite evidence that many former recipients have lost Medicaid, three-fourths of the money—$383 million—remained unspent.

Other incremental solutions fail repeatedly. At its heart, the problem is an almost mystical faith that competition and the free market will provide the best results. Upon his election in 1992, President Bill Clinton declared that the guiding principle of the health-care reform he would propose would be competition, but the problems we were facing had been created by competition; unbridled competition was the very illness.

The problems that competition creates could be seen plainly in 1992: lack of interest among providers and insurance companies in people who could not pay for care; increasing integration of providers, creating local monopolies; widespread fraud by providers; steeply rising costs; selective marketing of health insurance so that unprofitable classes of people could only get coverage at prohibitive cost; aggressive, sophisticated marketing that forced nonprofit and public hospitals to cut back and close their doors; and the dedication of as much as 15 to 25 or 30 percent of insurance premiums to corporate profit.

After the Clinton health-care plan went down in 1994—it would only have contributed to these structural pathologies anyway—these developments intensified. The once promising movement to HMOs has now largely been taken over by health-care corporations, which have cowed many physicians and medical societies and made visible the corporations' overriding interest in profits. In an article about these developments in *The New England Journal of Medicine* in 1999, Drs. Steffie Woolhandler and David Himmelstein wrote as follows:

Our main objection to investor-owned care is not that it wastes taxpayers' money nor even that it causes modest decrements in quality. The most serious problem with such care is that it embodies a new value system that severs the communal roots and Samaritan tradition of hospitals, makes doctors and nurses the instruments of investors, and views patients as commodities.[7]

Attentive citizens have seen ample evidence that this is so.

Targeted solutions such as a patient's bill of rights, insuring parents of children who are covered by the CHIP program, and requiring physicians and hospitals to report medical errors may produce pinpoint improvements, but will not deal with the broad problems of an uninsured population, inappropriate decisions about care, and the loss of patients' right to choose their physicians. Nor does it appear that a solution can be worked out for low- and moderate-income people alone. A broader solution is required.

The direct answer to these problems—an answer to which most legislators have so far seemed oblivious—is to declare every American eligible for health care, somewhat along the lines of Medicare. A government agency, an independent authority, or several regional authorities would administer such a program. The authorities would negotiate fee schedules with organizations of hospitals, and they would oversee capital construction to assure that it was necessary and did not duplicate facilities already available. Insurance companies would be allowed to cover only services not offered by the national plan.

Such an arrangement would make it feasible to plan the delivery of health care in relation to need rather than in terms of predatory advantage for one institution or another. Patients would be able to move freely from one physician or hospital to another. Systems like Medicaid and CHIP, with their apparatuses for checking eligibility, would disappear, and insurers would shrink or go out of business. An enormous amount of money would be saved and physicians could spend their time on the needs of their patients rather than in negotiation with HMOs and insurance company clerks.

One-seventh of the American economy is tied up in health care and one should not imagine that a sweeping change like this could be brought about readily. It would require an uprising by Americans, unwilling any longer to tolerate the chaotic, in some cases brutal, operation of our health care system.

If we do not want to take such a bold measure at one step, we might try it out with a national system that is limited to children, called Medicare for Children or, perhaps, Kiddiecare. Indeed, the program might begin with children under six years of age and move upward in age over a period of years. Children are the group that most needs coverage; yet they are, as it happens, the healthiest group and so the cheapest to cover. An outline of specifications for such a program is provided in Appendix C.

OTHER SIGNIFICANT AREAS

We shall not proceed encyclopedically through all the changes that would be required to reorient our economy and our society to achieve fairer shares and a basic reform of welfare. We will, however, name some important areas and the direction of change that would be required.

1. The Federal Reserve Board exercises commanding influence over the economy. Although it has been mandated by Congress to control inflation and assure full employment, when these two objectives appear to be in conflict, as they often do, the board is much more attentive to controlling inflation. It needs to regard both objectives with equal seriousness.

2. Housing is the major expenditure of low-income families. In addition to returning to a policy of substantially subsidizing moderate- and low-income housing, a broad solution must look to reorientation of financial institutions so that they promote the construction and rehabilitation of affordable housing.

3. Tax revenue must pay for many of the programs that we would wish to have—subsidizing the construction of moderate-income housing, extending the reach of health insurance, and so forth.

Since 1977, the burden of paying taxes has shifted from the wealthiest to middle- and lower-income people for these distinguishable reasons: individual tax rates have declined generally, but disproportionately at the upper end. Corporate taxes have assumed relatively less of the burden and individual taxes relatively more. There also has been, concurrently, a shift in balance from progressive income taxes to regressive payroll taxes (notably social security taxes) and, in state systems, from income taxes to sales taxes and user fees. Each of these shifts in itself transfers the tax burden from people with more income to people with less income.

For example, although tax rates have declined generally since 1977 they have declined more sharply for upper-income individuals, from a maximum of 50 percent to 39.6 percent today. In 1999, these cuts were worth an average of more than $40,000 to each of the one million most well-to-do families, according to Robert Greenstein of the Center on Budget and Policy Priorities.[8] As for corporation taxes, companies paid $60 billion less in income taxes in 1997 than they would have if they had paid at 1990 rates, but individuals paid $80 billion more.

Additional revenue, when needed, should come in the ways that draw revenue disproportionately from our richest citizens and businesses.

4. We should deal with the scores of technical-sounding provisions of social security and unemployment insurance programs, that have, over the past decades, been tweaked and revised to the disadvantage of lower-income people.[9] Much has changed and these provisions cannot simply be restored, but they should be reviewed and the bias against poor people reduced or eliminated. All

these details can be set right, coming as slowly as they went, as perhaps they should, if we set out on the course sketched here.

5. There is a need for a wide variety of social services for families and children, most strikingly the need for a nationwide network of high-quality child care providers.

6. Finally, as the unemployment rate is a bit above 4 percent at the time that this is written, it is difficult to discuss providing public employment at minimum wages or higher for people who cannot otherwise find work. These are people who are so handicapped in one way or another that they cannot find work in the private market or people who seek work in a time of economic downturn. Such a program was entertained by the designers of the 1996 welfare reform, but quickly rejected as inordinately expensive. Yet a recession will probably come at some time. It is well to keep in mind that such a program may be desirable.

It must be obvious that all these changes are interrelated. With higher wage levels, less would be required in income maintenance. Without universal entitlement to health care, much more would be required in wages or cash assistance. And so forth.

THE LADY, OR THE TIGER?

A short story written over a hundred years ago—a romantic fable, really—called "The Lady, or the Tiger?" by Frank Richard Stockton[10] might easily serve as a proposal for a television movie today. The story tells of a gallant young noble who has offended the king. He is to be tried in the customary way, placed in a vast amphitheatre, surrounded by encircling galleries of viewers. Exit is possible only through one of two doors. Behind one door waits a ravenous tiger, behind the other a beautiful lady, rich, of suitable age.

If he opens the door to the tiger, he will be fallen upon and consumed. If he opens the door to the lady, they will be married and presented with a castle and other riches. A princess who secretly favors the youth signals a clue about which door to choose, but he is not certain about her motives. Does she, he wonders, prefer that he die rather than see him married to someone else? We do not learn from the story how he chose or how it turned out.

A genre of social science fiction, best represented by authors such as Edward Bellamy, George Orwell, and H.G. Wells, describes the shape of a future society if we followed the road we were on or switched to another. Visionary when written, it is astonishing how prescient such works can turn out to be. Today, it does not take much imagination to see where our society is going: the future is implicit in the present. We know which door leads to the lady and which to the tiger; we have that advantage over Stockton's young noble.

In Chapter 7, in the tradition of Orwell and Wells but without claiming their talent, I have offered a fearful forecast. We do not need to go that way if we find it chilling to contemplate, or, we can continue on our road to a society that is affluent for some and barbaric for all. We can choose whether to open the door to the lady or the tiger.

NOTES

1. It may not entirely be a coincidence that the definition of poverty of these economists approximates public perceptions. Victor Fuchs' article in *The Public Interest* (no. 8, Summer 1967, p. 89) was based on his observation, over many years, that the level of income at which one is considered to be poor moves up in tandem with median incomes.

2. Richard B. Freeman and Laurence F. Katz, "Rising Wage Inequality: The United States vs. Other Advanced Countries" in Richard Freeman, ed., *Working Under Different Rules*. Russell Sage: New York, 1994.

3. Robert Cherry and Max B. Sawicky, "Giving Tax Credit Where Credit is Due." A Briefing Paper of the Economic Policy Institute: Washington, D.C., April 2000. Also, a personal letter from Max B. Sawicky to Alvin L. Schorr dated September 22, 2000.

4. In enhancing its child tax credit, the United States would join Great Britain, which is planning to introduce an "Integrated

Child Credit" in 2003. The British credit would provide a family benefit payable without regard to whether a family member is working; Australia and Canada have both "successfully" introduced such systems. An assessment of these new programs observes that "these benefits are higher for low-income families, but middle-income households with children also get some benefit. Such conditions have helped finance spending on children in ways that are relatively free of stigma and connotations with welfare." "Reforming Children's Benefits: International Comparisons." *Findings*, Joseph Rowntree Foundation: York, England. October 2000, P. 1.

5. Wayne Vroman, "The Effects of Welfare Reform on Unemployment Insurance," The Urban Institute: Washington, D.C. *Assessing the New Federalism*, Policy Brief no. 22, May 1998. See also Harry J. Holzer, "Unemployment Insurance and Welfare Recipients: What Happens when the Recession Comes?" The Urban Institute: Washington, D.C. no. A46, Dec. 2000.

6. Melissa B. Jacoby, Teresa A. Sullivan, and Elizabeth Warren, "Medical Problems and Bankruptcy Filings." Norton's Bankruptcy Advisor, May 2000.

7. Steffie Woolhandler and David Himmelstein. *The New England Journal of Medicine*, v. 341, no. 6, August 5, 1999. P. 446.

8. David Cay Johnston, "Gap Between Rich and Poor Found Substantially Wider." *New York Times*, September 5, 1999.

9. For example, after some years of uncertainty and debate, twenty years ago Congress wiped out the social security provision for a minimum benefit. The minimum benefit had assured $122 a month to those to whom the regular benefit calculation would have given less. At the time, a Social Security Administration study of who would lose from the change revealed that 80 percent were housewives—who had been employed fewer years than men, on the average. Now, recent work at the Urban Institute suggests the importance of reinstating the minimum benefit in order, in particular, to improve the circumstances of elderly lone women.

10. Frank Richard Stockton, *The Lady, or the Tiger?* Scribner: New York, 1884.

Appendix A: Statistical Tables and Charts

AFDC AND TANF

Table A-1
AFDC Summary Data, Selected Fiscal Years, 1936–1996

Measure	1936	1940	1950	1960	1970	1980	1990	1994	1995	1996
Benefit expenditures (millions of dollars) [a]	23	123	520	1,021	4,082	11,540	18,539	22,797	22,032	20,411
In 1996 dollars [b]	260	1,373	3,419	5,407	16,803	22,445	22,414	24,082	22,643	20,411
Federal share (percent)	7	33	44	60	54	54	55	55	55	54
Administrative cost (millions of dollars) [c]	0.4	9.5		109	881	1,479	2,661	3,301	3,521	3,266
In 1996 dollars [b]	4.5	106	263	577	3,627	2,877	3,217	3,487	3,619	3,266
Federal share (percent)	34	40	50	50	65	51	51	51	50	50

From "1998 Green Book," U.S. House of Representatives Ways and Means Committee Print, 1998, U.S. Government Printing Office Online via GPO Access, Document ID: f:wm007_07.105, Table 7.2. Source: Congressional Research Service.

[a] Benefit expenditures for 1936–60 are from U.S. Department of Health and Education (DHEW), Expenditures for Public Assistance Payments and for Administrative Costs, by Program and Source of Funds, Fiscal Years 1936–70 NCSS Report F-5; 1936 data are for 5 months only. Later data are from table 7-3, prepared by the U.S. Department of Health and Human Services (DHHS), but unlike that table, exclude foster care payments made in 1980.

[b] The Consumer Price Index (CPI-U) for all Urban Consumers was used to adjust current dollars for inflation.

[c] For years before 1980, administrative costs include some expenditures for services.

Table A–2

Total Unspent TANF Funds at the End of Federal Fiscal Year 1999 (in millions)

(All figures in millions)	Unobligated Funds As of 9-30-99	Unliquidated Obligations As of 9-30-99	Total Unspent Funds	Unspent Funds As a Percent of TANF Funds Available Since FY 1997
Alabama	$31.4	$4.8	$36.2	12%
Alaska	7.0	0	7.0	5
Arizona	0	91.3	91.3	13
Arkansas	0	39.5	39.5	29
California	0	1,620.6	1,620.6	15
Colorado	0	77.1	77.1	24
Connecticut	40.7	0	40.7	5
Delaware	0	2.9	2.9	3
District of Columbia	37.3	32.8	70.1	26
Florida	0	392.6	392.6	23
Georgia	119.7	16.1	135.8	14
Hawaii	4.0	1.4	5.4	2
Idaho	19.2	17.8	37.0	47
Illinois	0	0	0	0
Indiana	0	199.5	199.5	32
Iowa	21.0	5.7	26.7	7
Kansas	0	0	0	0
Kentucky	0	0	0	0
Louisiana	112.2	0	112.2	24
Maine	0	0	0	0
Maryland	47.2	52.1	99.3	15
Massachusetts	68.2	0	68.2	5
Michigan	146.1	0	146.1	6
Minnesota	66.7	67.3	134.0	21
Mississippi	73.2	20.5	93.7	35
Missouri	11.4	15.3	26.8	4
Montana	26.6	0	26.6	21
Nebraska	9.2	0	9.2	6
Nevada	0	16.8	16.8	13
New Hampshire	6.0	4.6	10.6	9
New Jersey	0	253.1	253.1	23
New Mexico	56.9	0	56.9	18
New York	752.1	370.8	1,122.9	16
North Carolina	3.4	98.3	101.7	12
North Dakota	8.3	0	8.3	16
Ohio	150.0	583.9	733.9	34
Oklahoma	61.4	0	61.4	14
Oregon	0	23.8	23.8	5
Pennsylvania	174.6	125.3	299.9	16
Rhode Island	0	0	0	0
South Carolina	0	32.2	32.2	11
South Dakota	11.9	2.2	14.0	23
Tennessee	103.6	19.6	123.2	21
Texas	0	175.6	175.6	12
Utah	17.8	0	17.8	8
Vermont	3.0	0	3.0	2
Virginia	1.7	14.2	15.9	4
Washington	130.2	68.1	198.3	18
West Virginia	153.5	0	153.5	51
Wisconsin	30.7	290.4	321.2	34
Wyoming	35.2	0	35.2	58

From "Welfare Balances After Three Years of TANF Block Grants: Unspent TANF Funds at the End of Fiscal Year 1999," by Ed Lazere, 2000, Center on Budget and Policy Priorities, p.14.

Table A–3
AFDC Summary Data, Selected Fiscal Years, 1936–1996

Measure	1936	1940	1950	1960	1970	1980	1990	1994	1995	1996
Average monthly no. (thousands) [a]										
Families	162	372	651	803	1,909	3,574	3,974	5,046	4,869	4,553
With unemployed parents	b	b	b	b	78	141	204	363	335	302
Recipients	546	1,222	2,233	3,073	7,429	10,497	11,460	14,226	13,619	12,649
Children	404	895	1,661	2,370	5,494	7,220	7,755	9,590	9,275	8,673
Average AFDC family size [c]	3.37	3.28	3.43	3.83	3.89	2.94	2.88	2.82	2.80	2.78
Average monthly family benefit	28	28	67	106	178	269	389	376	377	374
In 1996 dollars [d]	322	312	440	559	734	523	470	397	387	374
AFDC enrollment, as a percent of U.S. families with children	NA	2.1	3.2	3.1	6.6	11.5	12.3	14.8	14.2	13.3
Total population	0.4	0.9	1.5	1.7	3.7	4.6	4.6	5.5	5.2	4.8

Note. NA- not available. From "1998 Green Book," U.S. House of Representatives Ways and Means Committee Print, 1998, U.S. Government Printing Office Online via GPO Access, Document ID: f:wm007_07.105, Table 7.2. Source: Congressional Research Service.

[a] Enrollment data for 1936-60 are December numbers from the 1970 Social Security Annual Statistical Supplement (table 136). For later years data are fiscal year monthly averages from table 7-5, prepared by DHHS, but, unlike that table, exclude foster care recipients in 1980.

[b] Program did not exist.

[c] Calculated by dividing total recipients by the number of families. This understates actual family size for 1936-50 because the mother or other care giver was not included as a recipient until after fiscal year 1950.

[d] The Consumer Price Index (CPI-U) for all Urban Consumers was used to adjust current dollars for inflation.

Table A–4

Earnings and Benefits for a Mother of Two Children in Pennsylvania with Daycare Expenses After 4 Months on Job, January 1997

Earnings	EIC	AFDC [a]	Food Stamps [b]	Medicaid	Taxes			Work Expenses [d]	"Disposable" Income [e]
					Social Security	Federal Income [c]	State Income		
0	0	$5,052	$2,746	Yes		0	0	0	$7,798
$2,000	$800	4,892	2,434	Yes	$153	0	0	$600	9,373
4,000	1,200	3,292	2,554	Yes	306	0	0	1,200	9,540
5,000	2,000	2,492	2,614	Yes	383	0	0	1,500	10,223
6,000	2,400	1,692	2,674	Yes	459	0	0	1,800	10,507
7,000	2,800	892	2,734	Yes	536	0	0	2,100	10,790
8,000	3,200	0	2,822	Yes [f]	612	0	0	2,400	11,010
9,000	3,600	0	2,642	No [g]	689	0	0	2,700	11,853
10,000	3,656	0	2,462	No	765	0	0	3,000	12,353
12,000	3,641	0	2,102	No	912	0	0	3,600	13,231
15,000	3,009	0	1,562	No	1,148	0	$420	4,200	13,803
20,000	1,954	0	0	No	1,530	0	560	5,200	14,664
30,000	0	0	0	No	2,295	$1,560	840	5,400	19,905
50,000	0	0	0	No	3,825	4,944	1,400	5,400	43,431

From "1998 Green Book," U.S. House of Representatives Ways and Means Committee Print, 1998, U.S. Government Printing Office Online via GPO Access, Document ID: f:wm007_07.105, Table 7.3. Source: Congressional Research Service.

a Assumes these deductions: $120 monthly standard allowance (which would drop to $90 after 1 year on the job) and child care costs equal to 20 percent of earnings, up to maximum of $350 for two children.

b Assumes these deductions: 20 percent of earnings, $134 monthly standard deduction and child care costs equal to 20 percent of wages, up to maximum of $320 for two children. (If family also received the maximum shelter deduction, food stamp benefits would be $75 higher monthly.)

c Head of household rates for 1997. The dependent care tax credit reduces tax liability at earnings of $15,000 and above.

d Assumed to equal 10 percent of earnings up to maximum of $100 monthly, plus child care costs equal to 20 percent of earnings up to a maximum of $350 for two children.

e In addition, the benefits from Medicaid could be added, but are not, since the extent to which they increase disposable income is uncertain.

f Family would qualify for Medicaid for 12 months after leaving cash welfare. State must offer Medicaid to all children up to age 6 whose family income is not above 133 percent of the Federal poverty guideline (ceiling of $17,769 for a family of three in 1997) and to children over age 6 born after September 30, 1983 (up to age 13 in January 1997) whose family income is below the poverty guideline ($13,330 for a family of three).

g After losing her Medicaid transitional benefits, to regain eligibility mother must spend down on medical expenses to State's medically needy income limit ($5,604 for a family of three in September 1996).

Table A-5
Historic Trends in Average AFDC Payments and in Maximum Benefits for a Family of Four in the Median States, Current and Constant Dollars, a Selected Fiscal Years 1970–1996

	Fiscal Year								
AFDC Payments	1970	1975	1980	1985	1990	1992	1994	1995	1996
Average monthly benefit per family	$178	$210	$274	$339	$389	$389	$376	$377	$374
In fiscal year 1996 dollars	734	631	533	495	470	435	397	387	374
Average monthly benefit per person	46	63	94	116	135	136	134	135	134
In fiscal year 1996 dollars	189	189	183	169	163	152	142	139	134
Maximum benefit in July for a family unit of four with no income in the median State (ranked by benefit size) [b]	221	264	350	399	432	435	435	435	450
In fiscal year 1996 dollars	910	793	681	582	522	486	460	447	450

Note. AFDC benefit amounts have not been reduced by child support enforcement collections. From "1998 Green Book," U.S. House of Representatives Ways and Means Committee Print, 1998, U.S. Government Printing Office Online via GPO Access, Document ID: f:wm007_07.105, Table 7.7. Source: Family Support Administration, U.S. Department of Health and Human Services. Median State benefits provided by the Congressional Research Service (CRS). Table prepared by CRS.

[a] The constant dollar numbers were calculated by use of the Consumer Price Index for all Urban Consumers (CPI-U).

[b] Among the 50 states and the District of Columbia.

Table A–6
Maximum TANF Benefits by Family Size, July 1997

State	Maximum TANF benefit by size of filing unit					
	1	2	3	4	5	6
Alabama	$111	$137	$164	$194	$225	$252
Alaska	514	821	923	1,025	1,127	1,229
Arizona	204	275	347	418	489	561
Arkansas	81	162	204	247	286	331
California [a,b]	279	456	565	673	767	861
Colorado	214	280	356	432	512	590
Connecticut [a]	402	513	636	741	835	935
Delaware	201	270	338	407	475	544
District of Columbia	239	298	379	463	533	627
Florida	180	241	303	364	426	487
Georgia	155	235	280	330	378	410
Guam	420	537	673	776	874	985
Hawaii [b]	334	452	570	687	805	922
Idaho	276	276	276	276	276	276
Illinois [a]	212	278	377	414	485	545
Indiana	139	229	288	346	405	463
Iowa	183	361	426	495	548	610
Kansas [a]	267	352	429	497	558	619
Kentucky	186	225	262	328	383	432
Louisiana [a]	72	138	190	234	277	316
Maine	198	312	418	526	632	739
Maryland	167	295	377	455	527	579
Massachusetts [b]	383	474	565	651	741	832
Michigan: [a]						
Wayne County	276	371	459	563	659	792
Washtenaw	305	401	489	593	689	822
Minnesota	187	437	532	621	697	773
Mississippi	60	96	120	144	168	192
Missouri	136	234	292	342	388	431
Montana	266	358	450	542	633	725
Nebraska	222	293	364	435	506	577
Nevada	229	289	348	408	468	528
New Hampshire	414	481	550	613	673	754
New Jersey	162	322	424	488	552	616
New Mexico	231	310	389	469	548	627
New York: [a]						
New York City	352	468	577	687	800	884
Suffolk County	446	576	703	824	949	1,038

Table A-6 (continued)

North Carolina	181	236	272	297	324	349
North Dakota	228	340	490	528	604	667
Ohio	203	279	341	421	493	549
Oklahoma	190	238	307	380	445	509
Oregon	310	395	460	565	660	755
Pennsylvania [a]	215	330	421	514	607	687
Puerto Rico	132	156	180	204	228	252
Rhode Island	327	449	554	634	714	794
South Carolina	119	159	200	241	281	322
South Dakota	304	380	430	478	528	578
Tennessee	95	142	185	226	264	305
Texas	78	163	188	226	251	288
Utah	246	342	426	498	567	625
Vermont [a]	449	554	656	737	824	882
Virgin Islands	120	180	240	300	360	420
Virginia [a]	220	294	354	410	488	534
West Virginia	149	201	253	312	360	413
Wisconsin [a,c]	248	440	517	617	708	766
Wyoming	195	320	340	360	360	360
Median State [d]	215	310	379	463	528	590

From "1998 Green Book," U.S. House of Representatives Ways and Means Committee Print, 1998, U.S. Government Printing Office Online via GPO Access, Document ID: f:wm007_07.105, Table 7.47. Source: Congressional Research Service, on the basis of a telephone survey.

[a] These States (like Michigan and New York) have regional or urban/rural benefit schedules. Amounts shown are for highest benefit area.
[b] These States pay higher amounts than those shown above for persons exempt from work. See benefit schedule below.

State	Maximum TANF benefit by size of filing unit (exempt from work)					
	1	2	3	4	5	6
California	$311	$509	$631	$750	$855	$961
Hawaii	418	565	712	859	1,006	1,153
Massachusetts	392	486	579	668	760	854

[c] Effective September 1, 1997, Wisconsin scheduled statewide implementation of its W-2 (TANF) plan, which pays $555 monthly to all-size families in community service jobs and $518 to all-size families in "transitional" activities. Each missed hour of required activity reduces benefits by $4.25 per hour.

[d] Median State among 50 States and the District of Columbia, ranked by benefit size.

Table A–7
Monthly Benefit for a Single Parent with Two Children and No Income,
October 1997 and July 1996

State	1997 TANF Benefit	1996 AFDC Benefit	Change in Benefit
Alabama	$164	$164	nc
Alaska	923	923	nc
Arizona	347	347	nc
Arkansas	204	204	nc
California	565[a][*]	596[*]	($29)
Colorado	356[b]	356	nc
Connecticut	543[*]	543[*]	nc
Delaware	338	338	nc
District of Columbia	379	415	(36)
Florida	303[c]	303[c]	nc
Georgia	280	280	nc
Hawaii	712	712	nc
Idaho	276	317	(41)
Illinois	377[*]	377[*]	nc
Indiana	288	288	nc
Iowa	426	426	nc
Kansas	429[*][d]	429[*][d]	nc
Kentucky	262	262	nc
Louisiana	190	190	nc
Maine	418	418	nc
Maryland	388	373	15
Massachusetts	565[e]	565[e]	nc
Michigan	459[*]	459[*]	nc [f]
Minnesota	763[f]	532	[f]
Mississippi	120	120	nc
Missouri	292	292	nc
Montana	450	438	12
Nebraska	364	364	nc
Nevada	348	348	nc
New Hampshire	550[g]	550[g]	nc
New Jersey	424	424	nc
New Mexico	389	389	nc
New York	577[*]	577[*]	nc
North Carolina	272	272	nc
North Dakota	740[f]	431	[h]
Ohio	341	341	nc
Oklahoma	307	307	nc
Oregon	460	460	nc
Pennsylvania	403[*]	403[*]	nc
Rhode Island	554	554	nc
South Carolina	201	200	1
South Dakota	430	430	nc
Tennessee	185	185	nc
Texas	188	188	nc
Utah	426	426	nc
Vermont	611[*]	597[*]	14
Virginia	291[*]	291[*]	nc
Washington	546	546	nc
West Virginia	253	253	nc
Wisconsin	628[i]	517	111[j]
Wyoming	340[k]	360	(20)

Note. "nc" indicates no change. Numbers in parentheses indicate a reduction in benefits. From "One Year After Federal Welfare Reform: A Description of State Temporary Assistance for Needy Families (TANF) Decisions as of October 1997," by L.J. Gallagher, et. al., 1998, The Urban Institute, p. VI-2. Source: Urban Institute summary of state TANF decisions as of October 1997.

[*] Benefit varies by county or city within the state. The amount shown is the benefit level for the area containing the largest portion of the state population.
[f] TANF and food stamps are issued as a combined benefit.

[a] Amount shown is for non-exempt families.
[b] Amount shown is the basic benefit. Counties have the option to provide supplemental cash or non-cash assistance in addition to this amount.
[c] Amount shown is for families with shelter costs of at least $50. Families with lower shelter expenses receive a lower benefit.
[d] Amount includes a $135 shelter payment.
[e] Amount shown includes a rent allowance for families with shelter costs. Amount shown is for "non-exempt" families who are generally subject to the time limits and work requirements. The amount for exempt families is $579.
[f] Comparison of benefit levels is difficult because benefits under TANF include food stamps.
[g] Amount includes the maximum shelter allowance of $243.
[h] Comparison of benefit levels is difficult because benefits under TANF include food stamps.
[i] The amount shown is for participation in W-2 Transitions. The amount for participation in a Community Service Job is $673.
[j] Families participating in a Community Service Job receive $156 more a month than the 1996 benefit level.
[k] Amount shown is for families with shelter expenses.

118

Table A-8
AFDC Characteristics, Selected Years 1969–1995

Characteristic	May 1969	January 1973	May 1975	March 1979	1983[a]	1986[a]	1988[a]	1990[a]	1992[a]	1994[a]	1995[a]
Education of mother (percent of mothers):[b]											
8th grade or less	29.4	NA	16.7	9.5	NA	4.8	5.5	5.8	4.9	4.0	5.7
1-3 years of high school	30.7	NA	31.7	20.8	NA	14.3	14.7	16.5	18.8	17.6	16.5
High school degree	16.0	NA	23.7	18.8	NA	17.3	17.5	19.3	22.4	24.1	25.9
Some college	2.0	NA	3.9	2.7	NA	3.4	3.9	5.7	6.8	7.7	8.3
College graduate	0.2	NA	0.7	0.4	NA	0.5	0.6	0.4	0.5	0.5	0.6
Unknown	21.6	NA	23.3	47.8	NA	59.7	58.3	52.3	46.6	46.0	43.0
Age of mother (percent of mothers):[b]											
Under 20	6.6	NA	8.3[d]	4.1[c]	3.6[e]	3.3[e]	3.4[c]	7.9	7.6	6.3	6.1
20-24	16.7	NA	[d]	28.0[e]	28.6[e]	33.6[f]	32.2[f]	23.8[e]	24.5	24.6	24.6
25-29	17.6	NA	[d]	21.4	23.8	20.0[g]	19.4[g]	24.6	23.3	22.6	22.2
30-39	30.4	NA	27.9	27.2	27.9	30.1	31.5	32.0	32.7	34.9	34.9
40 or over	25.0	NA	17.6	15.4	15.7	13.0	13.4	11.7	11.8	11.5	12.2
Unknown	3.6	NA	3.0	4.0	0.3	-	-	-	0.1	-	-
Ages of children (percent of recipient children):											
Under 3	14.9	NA	16.5	18.9	22.5	21.9	21.1	24.2	24.6	23.8	22.3
3-5	17.6	NA	18.1	17.5	20.1	21.1	21.0	21.5	21.7	22.1	22.6
6-11	36.5	NA	33.7	33.0	31.5	32.4	33.3	27.5	32.4	31.7	32.7
12 and over	31.0	NA	30.9	29.8	25.5	24.3	22.4	21.3	21.2	22.2	22.0
Unknown	-	NA	0.8	0.9	0.3	0.1	1.3	0.0	0.0	0.3	0.3
Father's relationship to youngest child (percent):											
No father	NA	NA	NA	84.7	89.8	91.2	91.6	92.0	89.4	89.4	90.2
Natural father	NA	NA	NA	9.6	NA	NA	NA	NA	NA	NA	NA
Adoptive father	NA	NA	NA	0.0	NA	NA	NA	NA	NA	NA	NA
Stepfather	NA	NA	NA	5.6	NA	NA	NA	NA	NA	NA	NA

Note: NA- not available. In 1995, 1.8 percent of AFDC cases had zero children (they were expectant mothers). From "1998 Green Book," U.S. House of Representatives Ways and Means Committee Print, 1998, U.S. Government Printing Office Online via GPO Access, Document ID: Ewm007_07.105, Table 7.19. Source: Administration for Children and Families, U.S. Department of Health and Human Services.

[a] Data are for the Federal fiscal year October-September. All percentages are based on the average monthly caseload during the year. Hawaii and the territories are not included in 1983. Data for 1986 include Hawaii, but not the territories. Data after 1986 include the territories and Hawaii.
[b] For years after 1983, data are for adult female recipients.
[c] Under age 19.
[d] The percentage for 20-29 year olds was 43.1.
[e] The ages were 19-24 in 1979, 1983 and 1990.
[f] In 1986 and 1988 this age group was 19-25.
[g] In 1986 and 1988 this age group was 26-29.

Table A–9
AFDC Characteristics, Selected Years 1969–1995

Characteristic	May 1969	January 1973	May 1975	March 1979	1983[a]	1986[a]	1988[a]	1990[a]	1992[a]	1994[a]	1995[a]
Median months on AFDC since most recent opening	23.0	27.0	31.0	29.0	26.0	27.0	26.3	23.0	22.5	22.8	23.5
Race (percent of parents):[b]											
White	NA	38.0	39.9	40.4	41.8	39.7	38.8	38.1	38.9	37.4	35.6
Black	45.2	45.8	44.3	43.1	43.8	40.7	39.8	39.7	37.2	36.4	37.2
Hispanic	NA	13.4	12.2	13.6	12.0	14.4	15.7	16.6	17.8	19.9	20.7
Native American	1.3	1.1	1.1	1.4	1.0	1.3	1.4	1.3	1.4	1.3	1.3
Asian	NA	NA	0.5	1.0	1.5	2.3	2.4	2.8	2.8	2.9	3.0
Other and unknown	4.8	1.7	2.0	0.4	NA	1.4	1.9	1.5	2.0	2.1	2.2
Incidence of households (percent):											
Living in public housing	12.8	13.6	14.6	NA	10.0	9.6	9.6	9.6	9.2	8.3	8.0
Participating in food stamp or donated food program	52.9	68.4	75.1	75.1	83.0	80.7	84.6	85.6	87.3	88.6	89.0
Including nonrecipient members	33.1	34.9	34.8	NA	36.9	36.7	36.8	37.7	38.9	46.4	48.3

Note: NA – not available. In 1995, 1.8 percent of AFDC cases had zero children (they were expectant mothers). From "1998 Green Book," U.S. House of Representatives Ways and Means Committee Print, 1998, U.S. Government Printing Office Online via GPO Access, Document ID: f.wm007_07.105, Table 7.19. Source: Administration for Children and Families, U.S. Department of Health and Human Services.

[a] Data are for the Federal fiscal year October–September. All percentages are based on the average monthly caseload during the year. Hawaii and the territories are not included in 1983. Data for 1986 include Hawaii, but not the territories. Data after 1986 include the territories and Hawaii.
[b] For 1983, 12.6 percentage points where race was unknown were allocated proportionally across all categories.

Table A–10
Distribution of Time on AFDC for a Beginning Cohort of Recipients and for the Caseload at a Point in Time

Time on AFDC (months)	Beginning cohort-distribution of expected lifetime total	Current recipients	
		Distribution of expected lifetime total	Distribution of AFDC time to date
1-12	27.4	4.5	16.4
13-24	14.8	4.8	11.9
25-36	10.0	4.9	9.5
37-48	7.7	5.0	7.8
49-60	5.5	4.5	6.6
More than 60	34.8	76.2	47.8
Total	100.0	100.0	100.0
Average duration (years)	6.1	12.98	6.49

From "1998 Green Book," U.S. House of Representatives Ways and Means Committee Print, 1998, U.S. Government Printing Office Online via GPO Access, Document ID: f:wm007_07.105, Table 7.49. Source: Pavetti (1995).

Table A–11

AFDC Families by Reason for Deprivation of the Youngest Child, by State, Fiscal Year 1995
(in percentages except total families)

| State | Total Families | Parent Absent | | | | | | | | |
		Deceased	Parent Incapacitated	Parent Unemployed	Divorced or Legally Separated	Separated, but not Legally	Paternity Established Yes	Paternity Established No	Other Absence	Unknown
Alabama	46,030	0.7	1.9	0.1	13.1	8.6	23.3	48.5	2.2	1.7
Alaska	12,426	1.2	3.8	13.9	20.1	13.3	25.6	18.7	3.0	0.6
Arizona	69,609	1.3	4.0	1.3	12.3	16.8	21.4	39.3	2.1	1.5
Arkansas	24,296	1.7	4.5	1.1	14.8	10.4	27.8	34.3	2.8	2.5
California	919,471	2.1	4.7	16.1	9.6	10.8	15.0	36.1	4.6	0.9
Colorado	38,557	0.8	5.6	1.8	16.6	11.8	20.5	37.0	4.5	1.5
Connecticut	60,985	1.8	1.5	7.9	9.4	8.1	41.7	24.6	3.5	1.5
Delaware	10,775	1.9	1.9	0.0	14.5	5.9	45.1	26.2	3.4	1.2
District of Columbia	26,789	2.4	1.4	1.0	3.5	4.0	13.1	70.7	3.0	1.0
Florida	230,807	1.1	2.7	2.3	11.4	13.1	22.6	40.1	3.8	3.0
Georgia	139,135	1.7	2.6	0.8	11.1	11.7	62.2	7.4	1.3	1.3
Guam	2,099	0.6	3.0	7.9	10.6	4.2	34.5	32.7	5.1	1.2
Hawaii	21,674	2.3	5.1	6.7	11.8	15.8	18.8	36.0	3.0	0.5
Idaho	9,071	0.6	4.3	6.8	27.9	13.9	21.1	21.4	2.7	1.2
Illinois	236,205	1.0	1.1	5.0	7.4	11.2	16.9	53.5	2.6	1.3
Indiana	65,556	1.1	2.9	3.4	15.7	10.6	23.2	31.4	2.8	8.7
Iowa	36,435	0.7	2.9	9.1	23.8	7.9	30.7	22.5	1.4	1.2
Kansas	28,206	1.4	4.6	6.0	21.0	9.7	21.1	30.9	3.1	2.2
Kentucky	75,384	1.2	10.9	6.9	17.2	9.6	19.1	31.5	1.0	2.6
Louisiana	79,825	1.0	3.3	0.9	7.6	10.5	18.8	53.3	1.1	3.5
Maine	21,694	1.0	4.9	8.9	26.1	10.9	29.0	16.1	1.8	1.4
Maryland	77,677	1.1	1.0	0.8	5.6	6.9	29.9	33.4	11.1	10.2
Massachusetts	100,852	1.9	3.5	3.6	9.9	11.6	33.7	32.8	2.0	1.0
Michigan	201,696	1.4	1.9	8.0	11.7	7.0	28.7	31.1	4.0	6.3
Minnesota	57,061	1.3	3.7	6.9	18.4	7.9	32.3	26.5	1.6	1.6
Mississippi	52,528	1.2	3.6	0.0	6.4	16.2	25.7	44.4	1.5	1.1
Missouri	89,298	1.6	3.3	3.0	15.9	11.1	31.0	31.2	1.5	1.5

Montana	11,508	1.9	6.1	6.9	22.3	11.4	22.3	24.7	3.7	0.8
Nebraska	14,828	0.3	1.6	4.0	15.2	10.5	18.4	41.8	5.8	2.4
Nevada	15,708	1.0	0.7	3.0	14.2	18.2	18.7	39.6	4.5	0.2
New Hampshire	10,800	0.6	4.4	3.2	22.2	12.7	29.2	23.8	2.5	1.3
New Jersey	118,883	2.9	0.9	4.1	6.7	9.3	31.2	41.8	1.7	1.4
New Mexico	34,444	1.7	4.7	5.2	14.1	13.9	18.7	37.6	2.7	1.4
New York	456,929	1.6	2.9	5.1	7.2	14.2	38.6	20.6	4.1	5.7
North Carolina	125,503	1.2	2.3	1.8	10.5	10.8	29.5	38.3	3.0	2.6
North Dakota	5,215	2.0	3.6	1.6	22.7	3.3	43.4	18.4	3.2	1.6
Ohio	228,171	1.3	3.1	6.7	13.0	10.4	20.7	36.7	5.4	2.6
Oklahoma	44,790	0.9	3.8	0.1	23.6	15.5	17.0	36.7	1.4	0.9
Oregon	39,264	1.3	2.9	7.5	17.0	15.8	26.7	25.8	1.5	1.7
Pennsylvania	204,771	2.1	4.0	4.0	10.2	7.5	26.7	41.2	2.1	2.3
Puerto Rico	54,799	3.7	11.4	0.1	10.1	18.0	47.1	6.7	2.6	0.4
Rhode Island	22,194	1.7	3.0	3.4	12.8	19.9	29.8	27.2	0.6	1.7
South Carolina	48,981	1.1	3.1	0.6	8.2	18.0	27.6	38.9	0.1	2.6
South Dakota	6,286	2.0	3.9	0.7	19.3	7.2	31.0	31.7	2.3	2.0
Tennessee	104,009	1.9	4.4	2.1	16.1	11.9	23.2	35.4	3.3	1.9
Texas	274,505	2.4	3.7	2.0	10.8	19.1	11.3	47.7	2.3	0.8
Utah	16,648	0.7	6.5	0.9	25.0	15.7	16.0	28.6	5.1	1.5
Vermont	9,648	0.7	8.2	11.5	32.9	5.3	20.1	14.8	3.6	3.0
Virgin Islands	1,308	0.7	1.0	0.7	3.3	2.0	65.8	24.6	0.3	1.7
Virginia	72,147	1.0	2.8	0.4	9.7	14.9	25.6	41.8	2.2	1.8
Washington	101,949	1.6	4.3	14.3	15.2	12.0	24.2	23.4	3.6	1.5
West Virginia	38,404	0.7	10.8	14.5	19.4	15.9	14.8	21.2	1.4	1.4
Wisconsin	72,366	1.4	3.1	6.7	11.1	5.8	31.2	31.3	7.5	1.9
Wyoming	5,200	2.5	2.7	0.5	33.8	8.4	18.3	31.1	2.1	0.5
U.S. total	4,873,398	1.6	3.6	6.5	11.2	11.7	24.9	34.6	3.4	2.4

From "1998 Green Book," U.S. House of Representatives Ways and Means Committee Print, 1998, U.S. Government Printing Office Online via GPO Access, Document ID: f.wm007_07.105, Table 7.27. Source: Administration for Children and Families, U.S. Department of Health and Human Services.

Table A–12
Temporary Assistance for Needy Families Block Grant: Summary of Selected Major Provisions in State Plans

State	Maximum Time Before Mandatory Work	Time Limit on Benefits	Family Cap?	Benefit for Noncitizens?	Special Rules for Interstate Migrants?
Alabama	24 months	60 months	Did not say	No	No
Alaska	24 months	60 months	Did not say	Yes	No
Arizona	24 months	24 months within a 60 month period for adult recipients.	Yes	Yes	No
Arkansas	Did not say	24 months	Yes	Yes	No
California	Immediate	60 months	Yes	Yes	Yes
Colorado	24 months	60 months for adults	No	Yes	No
Connecticut	Did not say	21 months	Yes	Yes	No
Delaware	Immediate	48 months	Yes	Yes	No
District of Columbia	24 months	60 months	Did not say	Yes	Yes
Florida	Immediate	24 months in a 60 month period. Lifetime total of 48 months as a adult.	Yes	Yes	Yes
Georgia	24 months	Did not say	Yes	Yes	Yes
Guam	24 months	60 months	Did not say	No	No
Hawaii	24 months	60 months	Did not say	Yes	Yes
Idaho	With few exceptions, adults will be expected to participate in work activities immediately, including a job search requirement for all adult applicants.	24 months	Did not say	Yes	No
Illinois	24 months	60 months	Yes	Yes	No
Indiana	24 months	24 months	Yes	Yes	No
Iowa	Did not say	Individualized. TANF funds will not be used for an adult beyond 60 months unless the family meets criteria for extending assistance.	Did not say	Yes	No
Kansas	24 months	60 months	Did not say	Yes	No
Kentucky	24 months	60 months	Did not say	Yes	No
Louisiana	Did not say	24 months within a 60 month period.	Did not say	Yes	No
Maine	24 months	60 months	Did not say	Yes	No
Maryland	Did not say	60 months	Yes	Yes	Yes
Massachusetts	60 days	24 months within a 60 month period.	Yes	Yes	No
Michigan	24 months	60 months	Did not say	Yes	No
Minnesota	6 months; counties have the option of requiring work sooner	60 months	Did not say	Yes	Yes
Mississippi	24 months	60 months	Yes	No	No
Missouri	24 months	60 months, generally. JOBS mandatory recipients subject to self-sufficiency limit of 48 months.	Did not say	Yes	No
Montana	24 months	60 months	Did not say	Yes	No

State		Time limit			
Nebraska	Immediate participation in Job Support Program; earned income required within 2 years.	60 months	Yes	Yes	No
Nevada	24 months	60 months	Did not say	Yes	No
New Hampshire	Immediate job search for 26 weeks followed by 26 weeks of community work experience (cycle repeated each year).	60 months	Did not say	Yes	No
New Jersey	24 months	60 months	Yes	Yes	Yes
New Mexico	60 days	36 months	Did not say	Yes	No
New York	24 months	60 months	Did not say	Yes	Yes
North Carolina	Did not say	24 months at a time; lifetime maximum of 60 months.	Yes	Yes	No
North Dakota	24 months	60 months	Yes	Yes	Yes
Ohio	24 months	36 months plus a possible renewal of 24 months after 24 months of ineligibility (60 months over an 84 month period)	Did not say	Yes	No
Oklahoma	24 months	60 months	Did not say	Yes	No
Oregon	Did not say	24 months within an 84 month period.	Did not say	Yes	No
Pennsylvania	24 months	60 months	Did not say	Yes	Yes
Puerto Rico	24 months for participants determined not ready to work (lack high school diploma or equivalent). Participants who are ready to work will be engaged in work within 6 months.	Did not say	Did not say	Yes	No
Rhode Island	Participate in work or work-readiness activities within 45 days; work within 2 years.	60 months	Did not say	Yes	Yes
South Carolina	24 months	24 months out of 120 months; no more than 60 months in a lifetime.	Yes	Yes	No
South Dakota	24 months	18 months in a 60 month period.	Did not say	Yes	No
Tennessee	Immediate	60 month lifetime time limit.	Yes	Yes	No
Texas	Did not say	Did not say	Did not say	Yes	No
Utah	Immediate	36 months	Did not say	Yes	No
Vermont	Did not say	Did not say	Did not say	Yes	No
Virgin Islands	Did not say	60 months (for adult)	Did not say	Yes	No
Virginia	90 days	24 months within a 60 month period	Yes	Yes	No
Washington	Immediate job search required.	60 months	Did not say	Yes	Yes
West Virginia	24 months	60 months	Did not say	Yes	No
Wisconsin	Immediate	60 months	Yes	Yes	Yes
Wyoming	Did not say	60 months	Yes	Yes	No

Note: Information is from TANF State plans submitted to DHHS, supplemented by provisions in new State statutes of Arizona, California, New York, and Ohio. Some provisions may not be fully phased in. Some, notably, family caps and differential rules for interstate migrants, have been challenged in State courts. The family cap provision either prevents a family receiving welfare from getting additional benefits or provides the family with reduced benefits if they have additional children. Table is from CRS Report 97-380. From "1998 Green Book," U.S. House of Representatives Ways and Means Committee Print, 1998, U.S. Government Printing Office Online via GPO Access, Document ID: f:wm007_07.105, Table 7.44. Source Congressional Research Service (CRS).

125

Table A–13
Sanction Policies for Noncompliance with Work Activities Requirements

State	Initial Sanction [a]		Most Severe Sanction [b]	
	Amount of Sanction (Partial or Full Benefit Reduction)	Minimum Length of Sanction [c] (No. of Months)	Amount of Sanction (Partial or Full Benefit Reduction)	Minimum Length of Sanction [c] (No. of Months)
Alabama	Partial	*	Full	6
Alaska	Partial	1	Partial	12
Arizona	Partial	1	Full	1
Arkansas	Full [d]	*	Full [d]	3
California	Partial	*	Partial	6
Colorado [e]	Partial	1–3	Full	3–6
Connecticut	Partial	3	Full	3
Delaware	Partial	*	Full	Lifetime
District of Columbia	Partial	*	Partial	6
Florida	Full	*	Full	3
Georgia	Partial	1	Full	Lifetime
Hawaii	Partial	*	Partial	6
Idaho	Full	1	Full	Lifetime
Illinois	Partial	*	Full	3
Indiana	Partial	2	Partial	36
Iowa	Partial	3	Full	6
Kansas	Full	*	Full	2
Kentucky	Partial	*	Full	*
Louisiana	Partial	3	Full	*
Maine	Partial	*	Partial	6
Maryland	Full	*	Full	1 [f]
Massachusetts	Partial	*	Full	*
Michigan	Partial	1	Full	1
Minnesota	Partial	1	Partial	6
Mississippi	Full	2	Full	Lifetime
Missouri	Partial	*	Partial	6
Montana	Partial	1	Partial	12
Nebraska	Full	1	Full	12 [g]
Nevada	Partial	1	Full	Lifetime
New Hampshire	Partial	½	Partial	½
New Jersey	Partial	1	Full	3
New Mexico	Partial	*	Full	*
New York	Partial	*	Partial	6
North Carolina	Partial	3	Partial	12
North Dakota	Partial	1	Full	*

Table A-13 (continued)

Ohio	Full	1	Full	6
Oklahoma	Full	*	Full	*
Oregon	Partial	*	Full	*
Pennsylvania	Partial	1	Full	Lifetime
Rhode Island	Partial	*	Partial	*
South Carolina	Full	1 [h]	Full	1 [h]
South Dakota	Partial	1	Full	1
Tennessee	Full	*	Full	3
Texas	Partial	1	Partial	6
Utah	Partial	*	Full	*
Vermont	Partial	*	Full	*
Virginia	Full	1	Full	6
Washington	Partial	½ [i]	Partial	½ [i]
West Virginia	Partial	3	Full	6
Wisconsin	Partial/Full [j]	*	Full	Lifetime
Wyoming	Full	1	Full	1

From "One Year After Federal Welfare Reform: A Description of State Temporary Assistance for Needy Families (TANF) Decisions as of October 1997," by L.J. Gallagher, et. al., 1998, The Urban Institute, p. V-7. Source: Urban Institute summary of state TANF decisions as of October 1997.

* Length of sanction is until compliance.

[a] For comparison purposes, the initial sanction refers to the sanction a TANF recipient would receive if the recipient is non-compliant with work requirements for the first time and subsequently complies with the work requirement at the earliest possible time.

[b] The most severe sanction may go into effect after a subsequent instance of non-compliance or as a result of continual non-compliance after a specified length of time, depending on the state.

[c] The length of each sanction, unless otherwise specified, is the number of months stated or until the sanctioned recipient complies with the work requirements, whichever is longer.

[d] Arkansas: If the imposition of the sanction would result in the children in the home being removed to foster care, then the sanction for both first and subsequent instances of non-compliance is partial.

[e] Colorado: Counties have the option to set the length of sanction between 1-3 months for the initial sanction and between 3-6 months for the most severe sanction. Also, although the state has set the initial sanction as a partial benefit reduction, it has given counties the option of increasing this to a full benefit sanction.

[f] Maryland: The length of sanction is 1 month after compliance in contrast to 1 month or until compliance, whichever is longer.

[g] Nebraska: The length of sanction is 12 months or until the end of the 48 month Nebraska time-limit period, whichever is shorter.

[h] South Carolina: The length of sanction is 1 month after compliance in contrast to 1 month or until compliance, whichever is longer.

[i] Washington: The length of sanction is 2 weeks after compliance in contrast to 2 weeks or until compliance, whichever is longer.

[j] Wisconsin: If recipient works some of the assigned work hours, but fails to work all assigned work hours, the initial sanction is partial. If the recipient fails to work any of the assigned work hours, the initial sanction is full.

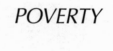

POVERTY

Table A–14
Poverty Thresholds in 1999, by Size of Family and Number of Related Children Under 18 Years

Size of family unit		Related Children Under 18 Years							
	None	One	Two	Three	Four	Five	Six	Seven	Eight or more
One person (unrelated individual)									
Under 65 years	8,667								
65 years and over	7,990								
Two persons									
Householder under 65 years	11,156	11,483							
Householder 65 years and over	10,070	11,440							
Three persons	13,032	13,410	13,423	16,954					
Four persons	17,184	17,465	16,895	19,882	19,578				
Five persons	20,723	21,024	20,380	22,964	22,261	21,845			
Six persons	23,835	23,930	23,436	26,595	25,828	24,934	23,953		
Seven persons	27,425	27,596	27,006	29,899	29,206	28,327	27,412	27,180	
Eight persons	30,673	30,944	30,387	36,169	35,489	34,554	33,708	33,499	
Nine persons or more	36,897	37,076	36,583						32,208

Source: U.S. Census Bureau, Current Population Survey

Table A–15

Number and Poverty Rate of All Persons and Families with Related Children under 18, by Race/Ethnicity (in thousands)

| | All Persons | | Families | | | | | | | |
| | | | All Families | | White | | Black | | Hispanic | |
Year	Percent	Number	Percent	Number	Percent	Number	Percent	Number	Percent	Number
1998	12.7%	34,476	15.1%	5,628	12.2%	3,665	30.5%	1,673	28.6%	1,454
1997	13.3%	35,574	15.7%	5,884	13.0%	3,895	30.5%	1,721	30.4%	1,492
1996	13.7%	36,529	16.5%	6,131	13.0%	3,863	34.1%	1,941	33.0%	1,549
1995	13.8%	36,425	16.3%	5,976	12.9%	3,839	34.1%	1,821	33.2%	1,470
1994	14.5%	38,059	17.4%	6,408	13.6%	4,025	35.9%	1,954	34.2%	1,497
1993	15.1%	39,265	18.5%	6,751	14.5%	4,226	39.3%	2,171	34.3%	1,424
1992r	14.8%	38,014	18.0%	6,457	14.0%	4,020	39.1%	2,132	32.9%	1,302
1991	14.2%	35,708	17.7%	6,170	13.7%	3,880	39.2%	2,016	33.7%	1,219
1990	13.5%	33,585	16.4%	5,676	12.6%	3,553	37.2%	1,887	31.0%	1,085
1989r	13.1%	32,415	15.7%	5,427	12.0%	3,344	35.4%	1,819	30.1%	1,071
1988r	13.0%	31,745	15.7%	5,373	11.9%	3,321	36.0%	1,802	29.7%	988
1987rr	13.4%	32,221	16.1%	5,465	12.3%	3,433	36.6%	1,788	31.9%	1,022
1986	13.6%	32,370	16.3%	5,516	13.0%	3,637	35.4%	1,699	30.8%	949
1985	14.0%	33,064	16.7%	5,586	13.3%	3,695	36.0%	1,670	32.1%	955
1984	14.4%	33,700	17.2%	5,662	13.4%	3,679	39.0%	1,758	31.3%	872
1983r	15.2%	35,303	17.9%	5,871	14.1%	3,859	39.9%	1,789	32.1%	867
1982	15.0%	34,398	17.5%	5,712	13.7%	3,709	40.7%	1,819	32.6%	802
1981	14.0%	31,822	15.9%	5,191	12.4%	3,362	37.1%	1,652	28.5%	692
1980	13.0%	29,272	14.7%	4,822	11.2%	3,078	35.5%	1,583	27.2%	655
1979r	11.7%	26,072	12.6%	4,081	9.2%	2,509	33.5%	1,441	24.6%	544
1978	11.4%	24,497	12.8%	4,060	9.3%	2,513	34.4%	1,431	24.1%	483
1977	11.6%	24,720	12.9%	4,081	9.6%	2,572	34.2%	1,406	25.3%	520
1976	11.8%	24,975	12.9%	4,060	9.6%	2,566	34.2%	1,382	27.2%	517
1975	12.3%	25,877	13.3%	4,172	10.3%	2,776	33.9%	1,314	29.1%	550
1974	11.2%	23,370	12.1%	3,789	9.0%	2,430	33.0%	1,293	25.2%	462
1973	11.1%	22,973	11.4%	3,520	8.2%	2,177	33.4%	1,280	23.8%	410
1972	11.9%	24,460	11.8%	3,621	8.4%	2,238	35.7%	1,303	24.5%	416
1971	12.5%	25,559	12.0%	3,683	8.9%	2,372	34.5%	1,261	na	na
1970	12.6%	25,420	11.6%	3,491	8.5%	2,219	34.9%	1,212	na	na
1969	12.1%	24,147	10.8%	3,226	7.9%	2,089	32.3%	1,095	na	na
1968	12.8%	25,389	11.4%	3,347	8.4%	2,176	34.6%	1,114	na	na
1967	14.2%	27,769	12.4%	3,586	8.9%	2,276	39.4%	1,261	na	na
1966	14.7%	28,510	13.4%	3,734	9.5%	2,400	na	na	na	na
1965	17.3%	33,185	15.6%	4,379	11.5%	2,858	na	na	na	na
1964	19.0%	36,055	16.9%	4,771	12.8%	3,205	na	na	na	na
1963	19.5%	36,436	17.6%	4,991	13.3%	3,328	na	na	na	na
1962	21.0%	38,625	19.4%	5,460	14.7%	3,673	na	na	na	na
1961	21.9%	39,628	19.9%	5,500	15.4%	3,785	na	na	na	na
1960	22.2%	39,851	19.7%	5,328	15.3%	3,690	na	na	na	na
1959	22.4%	39,490	-	-	-	-	-	-	-	-

Note. From 1979 onward, totals for families do not include unrelated subfamilies. An "r" indicates that data was revised by the Census Bureau. In 1987, data was revised twice. From "Poverty and Income Trends: 1998," by L. Rawlings, 2000, Center on Budget and Policy Priorities, p. 12, 25. Source: U.S. Bureau of the Census, Current Population Reports, unpublished data, March 1999 and prior reports.

Table A–16
Poverty in the World's Richest Nation

	Percentage of People in Poverty, [a] 1997		
	Under 50% of official poverty line	Under 100% of official poverty line	Under 150% of official poverty line
All persons	5.4	13.3	22.5
under 18	9.0	19.9	30.6
under 6	10.1	21.6	33.4
Male	4.7	11.6	20.0
Female	6.1	14.9	24.8
White	4.3	11.0	19.7
under 18	6.6	16.1	26.3
Black	12.2	26.5	39.8
under 18	19.8	37.2	51.7
Hispanic	10.9	27.1	43.9
under 18	16.0	36.8	55.8

[a] The poverty thresholds for 1997 were $8,183 for one person; $11,062 for a 2-person family with one adult and one child under 18; $12,919 for a 3-person family with one child; and $16,276 for a 4-person family with two adults and two children. Source: U.S. Bureau of the Census, *Poverty in the United States: 1997* (September 1998). From Chuck Collins, Betsy Leonard-Wright, and Holly Sklar, "Shifting Fortunes: The Perils of the Growing American Wealth Gap," (United for a Fair Economy: 1999) p. 29.

Table A–17
Program Participation Status of Poor Households (in thousands)

ALL RACES

Year	Received Means-Tested Assistance		Means-Tested Assistance Excluding School Lunches		Received Means-Tested Cash Assistance	
	#	%	#	%	#	%
1998	23,866	69.2%	20,496	59.5%	10,367	30.1%
1997	24,685	69.4%	21,830	61.4%	12,106	34.0%
1996	26,884	73.6%	23,520	64.4%	13,626	37.3%
1995	26,937	74.0%	23,904	65.6%	14,241	39.1%
1994	27,898	73.3%	24,949	65.6%	15,038	39.5%
1993	28,795	73.3%	25,992	66.2%	16,396	41.8%
1992r	27,958	73.5%	25,397	66.8%	16,241	42.7%
1991	26,034	72.9%	23,359	65.4%	15,566	43.6%
1990	24,031	71.6%	21,505	64.0%	14,040	41.8%
1989r	22,876	70.6%	20,023	61.8%	13,095	40.4%
1988	21,626	68.1%	19,065	60.1%	12,835	40.4%

Year	Received Food Stamps		Medicaid Coverage for 1 or More Persons		Living in Public or Subsidized Housing	
	#	%	#	%	#	%
1998	13,451	39.0%	17,363	50.4%	6,814	19.8%
1997	15,510	43.6%	18,935	53.2%	6,829	19.2%
1996	17,136	46.9%	20,366	55.8%	6,922	18.9%
1995	17,807	48.9%	20,635	56.7%	6,870	18.9%
1994	19,325	50.8%	21,329	56.0%	7,179	18.9%
1993	20,384	51.9%	22,260	56.7%	7,496	19.1%
1992r	19,588	51.5%	21,541	56.7%	7,029	18.5%
1991	17,920	50.2%	19,824	55.5%	7,183	20.1%
1990	16,375	48.8%	17,469	52.0%	6,667	19.9%
1989r	15,226	47.0%	15,898	49.0%	6,119	18.9%
1988	14,913	47.0%	14,942	47.1%	5,824	18.3%

WHITE

Year	Received Means-Tested Assistance		Means-Tested Assistance Excluding School Lunches		Received Means-Tested Cash Assistance	
	#	%	#	%	#	%
1998	15,006	64.0%	12,599	53.7%	5,971	25.5%
1997	15,747	64.5%	13,727	56.3%	7,201	29.5%
1996	16,995	68.9%	14,619	59.3%	7,644	31.0%
1995	16,755	68.6%	14,443	59.1%	7,671	31.4%
1994	17,091	67.3%	14,985	59.0%	8,380	33.0%
1993	17,710	67.5%	15,665	59.7%	9,034	34.4%
1992r	17,014	67.4%	15,116	59.8%	9,132	36.2%
1991	15,894	66.9%	13,969	58.8%	8,685	36.6%
1990	14,499	64.9%	12,659	56.7%	7,701	34.5%
1989r	13,455	63.2%	11,372	53.4%	6,824	32.0%
1988	12,533	60.5%	10,681	51.6%	6,706	32.4%

Year	Received Food Stamps		Medicaid Coverage for 1 or More Persons		Living in Public or Subsidized Housing	
	#	%	#	%	#	%
1998	7,921	33.8%	10,734	45.8%	3,372	14.4%
1997	9,573	39.2%	11,909	48.8%	3,677	15.1%
1996	10,182	41.3%	12,555	50.9%	3,415	13.9%
1995	10,321	42.3%	12,279	50.3%	3,117	12.8%
1994	11,149	43.9%	12,641	49.8%	3,292	13.0%
1993	11,983	45.7%	13,285	50.7%	3,507	13.4%
1992r	11,471	45.4%	12,824	50.8%	3,265	12.9%
1991	10,460	44.0%	11,625	49.0%	1,368	5.8%
1990	9,413	42.2%	10,106	45.3%	3,118	14.0%
1989r	8,349	39.2%	8,666	40.7%	2,816	13.2%
1988	8,047	38.8%	8,008	38.7%	2,790	13.5%

Table A–17 (continued)

BLACK

Year	Received Means-Tested Assistance		Means-Tested Assistance Excluding School Lunches		Received Means-Tested Cash Assistance	
	#	%	#	%	#	%
1998	7,502	82.5%	6,706	73.8%	3,786	41.6%
1997	7,511	82.4%	6,844	75.1%	4,179	45.8%
1996	8,371	86.4%	7,593	78.3%	5,120	52.8%
1995	8,614	87.3%	8,024	81.3%	5,629	57.0%
1994	9,001	88.3%	8,432	82.7%	5,721	56.1%
1993	9,509	87.4%	8,938	82.2%	6,427	59.1%
1992r	9,570	88.4%	9,028	83.4%	6,386	59.0%
1991	8,902	86.9%	8,296	81.0%	6,102	59.6%
1990	8,446	85.9%	7,915	80.5%	5,690	57.8%
1989r	8,229	86.4%	7,601	79.8%	5,489	57.6%
1988	7,842	83.8%	7,312	78.2%	5,369	57.4%

Year	Received Food Stamps		Medicaid Coverage for 1 or More Persons		Living in Public or Subsidized Housing	
	#	%	#	%	#	%
1998	4,734	52.1%	5,565	61.2%	3,111	34.2%
1997	5,094	55.9%	5,946	65.2%	2,792	30.6%
1996	6,052	62.4%	6,624	68.3%	3,102	32.0%
1995	6,477	65.6%	7,042	71.3%	3,454	35.0%
1994	7,046	69.1%	7,337	72.0%	3,513	34.5%
1993	7,434	68.3%	7,764	71.4%	3,682	33.8%
1992r	7,230	66.8%	7,638	70.5%	3,415	31.5%
1991	6,654	65.0%	7,223	70.5%	3,536	34.5%
1990	6,391	65.0%	6,544	66.5%	3,292	33.5%
1989r	6,077	63.8%	6,274	65.9%	2,996	31.4%
1988	6,070	64.9%	6,027	64.4%	2,724	29.1%

HISPANIC

Year	Received Means-Tested Assistance		Means-Tested Assistance Excluding School Lunches		Received Means-Tested Cash Assistance	
	#	%	#	%	#	%
1998	6,293	78.0%	4,975	61.6%	2,095	26.0%
1997	6,649	80.0%	5,433	65.4%	2,904	35.0%
1996	7,307	84.0%	5,933	68.2%	3,156	36.3%
1995	7,120	83.0%	6,069	70.8%	3,250	37.9%
1994	6,987	83.0%	5,815	69.1%	3,205	38.1%
1993	6,658	81.9%	5,447	67.0%	3,144	38.7%
1992r	6,238	82.2%	5,243	69.1%	3,031	39.9%
1991	5,207	82.1%	4,252	67.1%	2,510	39.6%
1990	4,661	77.6%	3,796	63.2%	2,301	38.3%
1989r	4,657	76.5%	3,541	58.2%	2,076	34.1%
1988	3,979	74.3%	3,104	57.9%	1,972	36.8%

Year	Received Food Stamps		Medicaid Coverage for 1 or More Persons		Living in Public or Subsidized Housing	
	#	%	#	%	#	%
1998	3,168	39.3%	4,295	53.2%	1,463	18.1%
1997	3,873	46.6%	4,893	58.9%	1,577	19.0%
1996	4,161	47.8%	5,357	61.6%	1,535	17.6%
1995	4,362	50.9%	5,422	63.2%	1,524	17.8%
1994	4,363	51.8%	5,098	60.6%	1,233	14.7%
1993	4,136	50.9%	4,853	59.7%	1,124	13.8%
1992r	3,918	51.6%	4,666	61.5%	1,144	15.1%
1991	3,189	50.3%	3,745	59.1%	1,056	16.7%
1990	2,829	47.1%	3,154	52.5%	984	16.4%
1989r	2,689	44.2%	2,829	46.5%	967	15.9%
1988	2,511	46.9%	2,376	44.4%	836	15.6%

Note. An "r" indicates that data was revised by the Census Bureau. From "Poverty and Income Trends: 1998," by L. Rawlings, 2000, Center on Budget and Policy Priorities, p. 41. Source: U.S. Bureau of the Census, Current Population Reports, unpublished data, March 1999 and prior reports.

Table A-18

Related Children Under 18 in Families Below 50% of the Poverty Level, by Race of Householder (in thousands)

Year	ALL RACES			WHITE			BLACK			HISPANIC		
	Number of All Children Under 18 in Poverty	Number of All Children <50% of Poverty	Children <50% of Poverty as % of All Poor Children	Number of White Children Under 18 in Poverty	Number of White Children <50% of Poverty	Children <50% of Poverty as % of All Poor Children	Number of Black Children Under 18 in Poverty	Number of Black Children <50% of Poverty	Children <50% of Poverty as % of All Poor Children	Number of Hispanic Children Under 18 in Poverty	Number of Hispanic Children <50% of Poverty	Children <50% of Poverty as % of All Poor Children
1998	12,845	5,355	41.7%	7,935	2,996	37.8%	4,073	1,944	47.7%	3,670	1,409	38.4%
1997	13,422	5,907	44.0%	8,441	3,326	39.4%	4,116	2,180	53.0%	3,865	1,657	42.9%
1996	13,764	5,854	42.5%	8,488	3,284	38.7%	4,411	2,267	51.4%	4,090	1,437	35.1%
1995	13,999	5,517	39.4%	8,474	3,008	35.5%	4,644	2,253	48.5%	3,938	1,561	39.6%
1994	14,610	6,442	44.1%	8,826	3,452	39.1%	4,787	2,573	53.7%	3,956	1,615	40.8%
1993	14,961	6,534	43.7%	9,123	3,368	36.9%	5,030	2,847	56.6%	3,666	1,261	34.4%
1992r	14,521	6,641	45.7%	8,752	3,423	39.1%	5,015	2,916	58.1%	3,440	1,302	37.8%
1991	13,658	6,022	44.1%	8,316	3,082	37.1%	4,637	2,585	55.7%	2,977	1,075	36.1%
1990	12,715	5,286	41.6%	7,695	2,855	37.1%	4,411	2,227	50.5%	2,750	986	35.9%
1989r	12,541	5,079	40.5%	7,450	2,610	35.0%	4,460	2,270	50.9%	2,824	952	33.7%
1988	11,935	5,372	45.0%	7,095	2,798	39.4%	4,148	2,308	55.6%	2,576	1,071	41.6%
1987	12,435	5,434	43.7%	7,550	3,013	39.9%	4,297	2,196	51.1%	na	na	na
1986	12,257	5,191	42.4%	7,714	2,834	36.7%	4,039	2,193	54.3%	na	na	na
1985	12,483	5,027	40.3%	7,838	2,819	36.0%	4,057	2,019	49.8%	na	na	na
1984	12,929	5,358	41.4%	8,086	2,997	37.1%	4,320	2,166	50.1%	na	na	na
1983	13,427	5,618	41.8%	8,534	3,257	38.2%	4,273	2,155	50.4%	na	na	na
1982	13,139	5,287	40.2%	8,282	3,003	36.3%	4,388	2,126	48.5%	na	na	na
1981	12,068	4,543	37.6%	7,429	2,492	33.5%	4,170	1,905	45.7%	na	na	na
1980	11,114	4,075	36.7%	6,817	2,309	33.9%	3,906	1,619	41.4%	na	na	na
1979	9,993	3,398	34.0%	5,909	1,852	31.3%	3,745	1,421	37.9%	na	na	na
1978	9,722	3,274	33.7%	5,674	1,778	31.3%	3,781	1,426	37.7%	na	na	na
1977	10,028	3,204	32.0%	5,943	1,876	31.6%	3,850	1,265	32.9%	na	na	na
1976	10,081	2,811	27.9%	6,034	1,712	28.4%	3,758	1,052	28.0%	na	na	na
1975	10,882	3,426	31.5%	6,748	2,013	29.8%	3,884	1,351	34.8%	na	na	na

Note. From 1979 onward, totals for families do not include unrelated subfamilies. An "r" indicates that data was revised by the Census Bureau. From "Poverty and Income Trends: 1998," by L. Rawlings, 2000, Center on Budget and Policy Priorities, p. 53. Source: U.S. Bureau of the Census, Current Population Reports, unpublished data, March 1999 and prior reports.

Table A–19
Number of Poor Children Before and After Counting Government Benefits and Taxes

	Number of Poor Children (in thousands)		Child Poverty Rate	
	Before counting government benefits and taxes	After counting government benefits and taxes	Before counting government benefits and taxes	After counting government benefits and taxes
1993	18,198	13,853	26.3%	20.0%
1995	17,098	11,443	24.2%	16.2%
1998	15,365	10,230	21.5%	14.3%
Change:				
1993-1995	-1,100	-2,410	-2.1% pts.	-3.8% pts.
1995-1998	-1,733	-1,213	-2.7% pts.	-1.9% pts.
Average Annual Change:				
1993-1995	-550	-1,205	-1.1% pts.	-1.9% pts.
1995-1998	-578	-404	-0.9% pts.	-0.6% pts.

From "Recent Changes in the Impact of the Safety Net on Child Poverty," by K. Porter, W. Primus, 1999, Center on Budget and Policy Priorities, p. 4. Source: U.S. Bureau of the Census, Current Population Survey.

Table A–20

Impact of Safety Net on All Children for Selected Years, 1979–1998

	1979	1983	1989	1993	1994	1995	1996	1997	1998
Total Child Population (thousands)	63,375	62,333	65,602	69,292	70,020	70,566	70,650	71,069	71,338
Number of Poor Children (thousands):									
Before counting government benefits and taxes	12,761	16,146	14,954	18,198	17,828	17,098	16,642	16,294	15,365
Plus social insurance	11,364	14,405	13,846	16,685	16,324	15,717	15,426	14,890	14,131
Plus cash assistance based on income	10,377	13,911	13,154	15,727	15,289	14,665	14,463	14,113	13,467
Plus food and housing benefits	8,421	12,464	11,409	13,874	13,212	12,476	12,576	12,511	11,749
Less federal taxes plus EITC	8,620	13,293	11,811	13,853	12,613	11,443	11,341	11,080	10,230
Child Poverty Rate (in percent):									
Before counting government benefits and taxes	20.1	25.9	22.8	26.3	25.5	24.2	23.6	22.9	21.5
Plus social insurance	17.9	23.1	21.1	24.1	23.3	22.3	21.8	21.0	19.8
Plus cash assistance based on income	16.4	22.3	20.1	22.7	21.8	20.8	20.5	19.9	18.9
Plus food and housing benefits	13.3	20.0	17.4	20.0	18.9	17.7	17.8	17.6	16.5
Less federal taxes plus EITC	13.6	21.3	18.0	20.0	18.0	16.2	16.1	15.6	14.3
Number of Children Removed from Poverty Due to (thousands):									
Social insurance	1,397	1,741	1,108	1,513	1,504	1,381	1,216	1,404	1,234
Cash assistance based on income	987	494	692	958	1,035	1,052	963	777	664
Food and housing benefits	1,956	1,447	1,745	1,853	2,077	2,189	1,887	1,602	1,718
Federal taxes plus EITC	(199)	(829)	(402)	21	599	1,033	1,235	1,431	1,519
Total	4,141	2,853	3,143	4,345	5,215	5,655	5,301	5,214	5,135
Percent of Children Removed from Poverty:									
Social insurance	10.9	10.8	7.4	8.3	8.4	8.1	7.3	8.6	8.0
Cash assistance based on income	7.7	3.1	4.6	5.3	5.8	6.2	5.8	4.8	4.3
Food and housing benefits	15.3	9.0	11.7	10.2	11.7	12.8	11.3	9.8	11.2
Federal taxes plus EITC	(1.6)	(5.1)	(2.7)	0.1	3.4	6.0	7.4	8.8	9.9
Total	32.5	17.7	21.0	23.9	29.3	33.1	31.9	32.0	33.4
Percentage Point Reduction in Poverty Rate Due to:									
Social insurance	2.2	2.8	1.7	2.2	2.1	2.0	1.7	2.0	1.7
Cash assistance based on income	1.6	0.8	1.1	1.4	1.5	1.5	1.4	1.1	0.9
Food and housing benefits	3.1	2.3	2.7	2.7	3.0	3.1	2.7	2.3	2.4
Federal taxes plus EITC	(0.3)	(1.3)	(0.6)	0.0	0.9	1.5	1.7	2.0	2.1
Total	6.5	4.6	4.8	6.3	7.4	8.0	7.5	7.3	7.2

From "Recent Changes in the Impact of the Safety Net on Child Poverty," by K. Porter, W. Primus, 1999, Center on Budget and Policy Priorities, Table A-1. Source: U.S. Bureau of the Census, unpublished data.

Table A–21
Work Experience of Poor Persons (in thousands)

Year	Number of Poor 16+ Years Old [a]	Number Who Worked	Percent Who Worked	Number of Poor Who Worked Less Than Full-Time Year-Round	Percent of Poor Who Worked Less Than Full-Time Year-Round	Number of Poor Who Worked Full-Time Year-Round	Percent of Poor Who Worked Full-Time Year-Round
1998	22,255	9,133	41.0%	6,330	28.4%	2,804	12.6%
1997	22,754	9,444	41.5%	7,098	31.2%	2,345	10.3%
1996	23,472	9,586	40.8%	7,322	31.2%	2,263	9.6%
1995	23,077	9,484	41.1%	7,066	30.6%	2,418	10.5%
1994	24,108	9,829	40.8%	7,309	30.3%	2,520	10.5%
1993	24,832	10,144	40.9%	7,737	31.2%	2,408	9.7%
1992r	23,951	9,739	40.7%	7,529	31.4%	2,211	9.2%
1991	22,498	9,175	40.8%	7,099	31.6%	2,076	9.2%
1990	21,198	8,675	40.9%	6,637	31.3%	2,038	9.6%
1989r	20,316	8,566	42.2%	6,649	32.7%	1,917	9.4%
1988r	20,911	8,474	40.5%	6,545	31.3%	1,929	9.2%
1987rr	21,161	8,347	39.4%	6,526	30.8%	1,821	8.6%
1986	21,352	8,864	41.5%	6,855	32.1%	2,009	9.4%
1985	21,954	9,112	41.5%	7,140	32.5%	1,972	9.0%
1984	22,246	9,104	40.9%	7,028	31.6%	2,076	9.3%
1983	23,465	9,434	40.2%	7,369	31.4%	2,065	8.8%
1982	22,812	9,119	40.0%	7,119	31.2%	2,000	8.8%
1981	21,260	8,631	40.6%	6,748	31.7%	1,883	8.9%
1980	19,517	7,792	39.9%	6,146	31.5%	1,646	8.4%
1979	16,833	6,504	38.6%	5,155	30.6%	1,349	8.0%
1978	16,914	6,599	39.0%	5,290	31.3%	1,309	7.7%
1977	16,864	6,459	38.3%	5,001	29.7%	1,458	8.6%
1976	16,994	6,555	38.6%	5,200	30.6%	1,355	8.0%
1975	17,300	6,697	38.7%	5,381	31.1%	1,316	7.6%
1974	16,132	6,376	39.5%	4,797	29.7%	1,579	9.8%
1973	15,428	6,186	40.1%	4,753	30.8%	1,433	9.3%
1972	16,393	6,329	38.6%	4,795	29.3%	1,534	9.4%
1971	17,197	6,836	39.8%	5,154	30.0%	1,682	9.8%
1970	16,981	6,716	39.6%	5,092	30.0%	1,624	9.6%
1969	16,288	6,469	39.7%	4,798	29.5%	1,671	10.3%
1968	16,673	7,146	42.9%	5,020	30.1%	2,126	12.8%
1967	18,403	7,927	43.1%	5,557	30.2%	2,370	12.9%
1966	18,474	8,085	43.8%	5,596	30.3%	2,489	13.5%

Note. An "r" indicates that data was revised by the Census Bureau. In 1987, data was revised twice. From "Poverty and Income Trends: 1998," by L. Rawlings, 2000, Center on Budget and Policy Priorities, p. 83. Source: U.S. Bureau of the Census, Current Population Reports, unpublished data, March 1999 and prior reports.

[a] Between 1966 and 1978, includes persons 14 years of age and older. Between 1979 and 1989, includes persons 15 years of age and older. From 1990 onward, includes persons 16 years of age and older.

Table A–22
Poverty Among Families with Children Where the Householder Worked

Year	Number of Poor Families with Children, Householder Worked (Millions)	Poverty Rate
1998	3.48	10.9%
1997	3.51	10.9%
1996	3.48	10.9%
1995	3.35	10.6%
1994	3.62	11.1%
1993	3.61	11.4%
1992r	3.55	11.3%
1991	3.37	11.2%
1990	3.18	10.5%
1989r	3.02	10.0%
1988r	2.94	9.8%
1987rr	2.84	9.7%
1986	2.96	10.1%
1985	3.03	10.5%
1984	3.01	10.6%
1983r	3.15	11.2%
1982	3.06	10.9%
1981	2.88	10.1%
1980	2.62	9.1%
1979	2.18	7.7%
1978	2.18	7.8%
1977	2.16	7.7%
1976	2.11	7.6%
1975	2.29	8.3%

Note. An "r" indicates that data was revised by the Census Bureau. In 1987, data was revised twice. From "Poverty and Income Trends: 1998," by L. Rawlings, 2000, Center on Budget and Policy Priorities, p. 85. Source: U.S. Bureau of the Census, Current Population Reports, unpublished data, March 1999 and prior reports.

Table A–23

Amount by Which the Earnings of a Family with One Full-Time Minimum-Wage Worker Fall Below the Poverty Line, by Family Size (in 1998 CPI-U-XI dollars)

Year	Annual Income from full-time work at the minimum wage	Family of Four			Family of Three		
		Poverty line	Amount below (or above) poverty for family with one earner at minimum wage	Earnings as % of poverty line for a family of four	Poverty line	Amount below (or above) poverty for family with one earner at minimum wage	Earnings as % of poverty line for a family of three
1998	$10,712	$16,660	$5,948	64.3%	$13,003	$2,291	82.4%
1997	10,315	16,813	6,498	61.4%	12,750	2,434	80.9%
1996	9,454	16,659	7,206	56.7%	13,003	3,549	72.7%
1995	9,455	16,652	7,197	56.8%	13,004	3,549	72.7%
1994	9,723	16,653	6,930	58.4%	13,002	3,279	74.8%
1993	9,972	16,653	6,681	59.9%	12,997	3,025	76.7%
1992	10,270	16,654	6,384	61.7%	12,996	2,726	79.0%
1991	10,579	16,664	6,084	63.5%	12,997	2,417	81.4%
1990	9,565	16,660	7,095	57.4%	12,994	3,428	73.6%
1989	9,160	16,660	7,501	55.0%	12,994	3,834	70.5%
1988	9,601	16,661	7,060	57.6%	13,000	3,399	73.9%
1987	9,998	16,660	6,662	60.0%	12,994	2,996	76.9%
1986	10,363	16,661	6,298	62.2%	12,994	2,631	79.8%
1985	10,556	16,647	6,091	63.4%	12,987	2,431	81.3%
1984	10,932	16,644	5,712	65.7%	12,985	2,054	84.2%
1983	11,403	16,657	5,253	68.5%	12,991	1,587	87.8%
1982	11,881	16,815	4,934	70.7%	13,117	1,236	90.6%
1981	12,606	16,801	4,195	75.0%	13,116	510	96.1%
1980	12,771	16,664	3,894	76.6%	13,002	232	98.2%
1979	13,287	16,326	3,040	81.4%	12,740	(546)	104.3%
1978	13,310	16,087	2,777	82.7%	12,559	(751)	106.0%
1977	12,338	15,967	3,629	77.3%	12,465	126	99.0%
1976	12,557	15,957	3,400	78.7%	12,458	(99)	100.8%
1975	12,065	15,952	3,886	75.6%	12,451	386	96.9%
Change: 1980/98	($2,059)		$2,054			$2,203	

Note: "Full-time" earnings are based on 40 hours of work for 52 weeks a year. From "Poverty and Income Trends: 1998," by L. Rawlings, 2000, Center on Budget and Policy Priorities, p. 86. Source: U.S. Bureau of the Census, Current Population Reports, unpublished data, March 1999 and prior reports.

Table A–24
Number and Percent of Persons with No Health Insurance (in millions)

Year	All Persons		All Poor Persons		All Persons <18		All Poor Persons <18	
	Percent	Number	Percent	Number	Percent	Number	Percent	Number
1998	16.2%	43.9	32.3%	11.2	15.0%	10.7	25.2%	3.4
1997	16.1%	43.2	31.6%	11.2	14.8%	10.5	23.8%	3.4
1996	15.6%	41.5	30.8%	11.3	14.6%	10.3	23.3%	3.4
1995	15.3%	40.4	30.2%	11.0	13.6%	9.6	21.4%	3.1
1994	15.2%	39.7	29.1%	11.1	14.1%	9.8	21.8%	3.3
1993	15.3%	39.7	29.3%	11.5	12.6%	8.6	20.1%	3.2
1992r	14.7%	37.4	28.5%	10.5	12.4%	8.3	20.3%	3.1
1991	14.1%	35.4	28.6%	10.2	12.6%	8.3	20.5%	2.9
1990	13.9%	34.6	28.6%	9.6	12.9%	8.4	21.8%	2.9
1989r	13.9%	34.5	30.6%	9.9	13.3%	8.5	25.1%	3.3
1988	13.4%	32.6	30.6%	9.7	13.0%	8.3	25.4%	3.2
1987	12.9%	31.0						

Note. An "r" indicates that data was revised by the Census Bureau. The Census Bureau made changes in the methods by which information on health insurance coverage was collected for 1994. The main refinement resulted in more people with employer-related coverage being identified. Also, the refined data collection methodology for 1994 is likely to understate the increase in the number of people without health insurance over time. From "Poverty and Income Trends: 1998," by L. Rawlings, 2000, Center on Budget and Policy Priorities, p. 97. Source: U.S. Bureau of the Census, Current Population Reports, unpublished data, March 1999 and prior reports.

*EARNINGS AND INCOME
DISTRIBUTION*

Table A-25

Average Gross Weekly Earnings of Nonsupervisory or Production Workers on Private Nonagricultural Payrolls (in 1998 CPI-X dollars)

Year	Current Dollars	1998 Dollars
1998	$442.19	$442.19
1997	424.89	431.51
1996	406.61	422.42
1995	394.34	421.77
1994	385.86	424.39
1993	373.64	421.48
1992	363.61	422.44
1991	353.98	423.63
1990	345.35	430.70
1989	334.24	439.36
1988	322.02	443.70
1987	312.50	448.39
1986	304.85	453.38
1985	299.09	453.08
1984	292.86	459.44
1983	280.70	459.38
1982	267.26	455.68
1981	255.20	461.68
1980	235.10	465.63
1979	219.91	484.40
1978	203.70	491.90
1977	189.00	487.45
1976	175.45	481.45
1975	163.53	474.30
1974	154.76	486.05
1973	145.39	502.09
1972	136.90	502.58
1971	127.31	481.47
1970	119.83	472.94
1969	114.61	474.15
1968	107.73	465.78
1967	101.84	457.30
1966	98.82	457.60
1965	95.45	454.92
1964	91.33	441.74
1963	88.46	433.00
1962	85.91	426.93
1961	82.60	414.27
1960	80.67	408.36
1959	78.78	406.37
1958	75.08	389.75
1957	73.33	391.89
1956	70.74	389.55
1955	67.72	379.33
1954	64.52	360.16
1953	63.76	358.38
1952	60.65	343.26
1951	57.86	333.26
1950	53.13	330.54

From "Poverty and Income Trends: 1998," by L. Rawlings, 2000, Center on Budget and Policy Priorities, p. 93. Source: Bureau of Labor Statistics, Employment and Earnings, June 1999, Table B-2, and prior reports.

Table A–26
Average Hourly Earnings of Nonsupervisory or Production Workers on Private
Nonagricultural Payrolls (in 1998 CPI-X dollars)

Year	Current Dollars	1998 Dollars
1998	$12.78	$12.78
1997	12.28	12.47
1996	11.82	12.28
1995	11.43	12.23
1994	11.12	12.23
1993	10.83	12.22
1992r	10.57	12.28
1991	10.32	12.35
1990	10.01	12.48
1989	9.66	12.70
1988	9.28	12.79
1987	8.98	12.89
1986	8.76	13.03
1985	8.57	12.98
1984	8.32	13.05
1983	8.02	13.13
1982	7.68	13.09
1981	7.25	13.12
1980	6.66	13.19
1979	6.16	13.57
1978	5.69	13.74
1977	5.25	13.54
1976	4.86	13.34
1975	4.53	13.14
1974	4.24	13.32
1973	3.94	13.61
1972	3.70	13.58
1971	3.45	13.05
1970	3.23	12.75
1969	3.04	12.58
1968	2.85	12.32
1967	2.68	12.03
1966	2.56	11.85
1965	2.46	11.72
1964	2.36	11.41
1963	2.28	11.16
1962	2.22	11.03
1961	2.14	10.73
1960	2.09	10.58
1959	2.02	10.42
1958	1.95	10.12
1957	1.89	10.10
1956	1.80	9.91
1955	1.71	9.58
1954	1.65	9.21
1953	1.61	9.05
1952	1.52	8.60
1951	1.45	8.35
1950	1.34	8.31

Note. An "r" indicates that data was revised. From "Poverty and Income Trends: 1998," by L. Rawlings, 2000, Center on Budget and Policy Priorities, p. 94. Source: Bureau of Labor Statistics, Employment and Earnings, June 1999, Table B-2, and prior reports.

Table A–27
Shifting Family Incomes

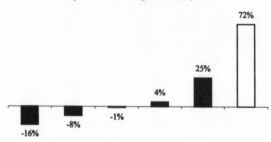

Change in After-Tax Income of Families, 1977-94

72%

25%

4%

-1%

-8%

-16%

Bottom 20%   Second 20%   Middle 20%   Fourth 20%   Top 20%   Top 1%

	Average After-Tax Income in 1994		
Income Class	Actual	If share of national income was the same as in 1977	The Difference
Bottom 20%	$7,175	$9,829	$2,654
Second 20%	$16,540	$19,352	$2,812
Middle 20%	$25,651	$27,448	$1,797
Fourth 20%	$37,226	$39,129	$1,903
Top 20%	$80,417	$71,736	-$8,681
Top 1%	$374,131	$241,176	-$132,955

<u>Note</u>. Table reflects income after federal taxes. Because state and local taxes are even more regressive, the picture would show more inequality if they were included. Source: Isaac Shapiro and Robert Greenstein, "Trends in the Distribution of After-Tax Income: An Analysis of Congressional Budget Office Data," Center on Budget and Policy Priorities, Washington, DC, August 14, 1997. From Chuck Collins, Betsy Leonard-Wright, and Holly Sklar, "Shifting Fortunes: The Perils of the Growing American Wealth Gap," (United for a Fair Economy: 1999) p. 31.

Table A–28
The Wage Gap

CEO Pay as a Multiple of Average Factory Worker Pay

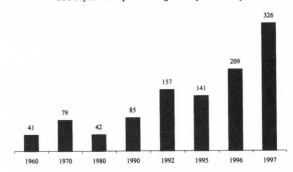

Source: *Business Week*, annual reports on executive pay. From Chuck Collins, Betsy Leonard-Wright, and Holly Sklar, "Shifting Fortunes: The Perils of the Growing American Wealth Gap," (United for a Fair Economy: 1999) p. 32.

Table A–29
Saving Less and Less

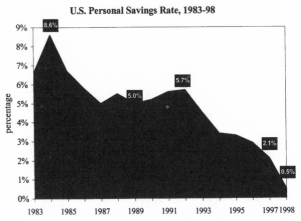

<u>Note</u>. Figures are for personal savings as a percentage of disposable personal income. Source: U.S. Department of Commerce, Bureau of Economic Analysis. From Chuck Collins, Betsy Leonard-Wright, and Holly Sklar, "Shifting Fortunes: The Perils of the Growing American Wealth Gap," (United for a Fair Economy: 1999) p. 43.

Table A–30
The Racial Wealth Gap

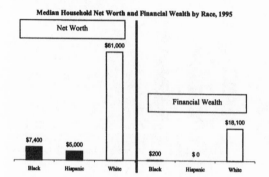

Median Household Net Worth and Financial Wealth by Race, 1995

Net Worth — Black $7,400; Hispanic $5,000; White $61,000

Financial Wealth — Black $200; Hispanic $0; White $18,100

Note. Financial wealth is net worth minus net equity in owner-occupied housing. Source: Edward Wolff, "Recent Trends in Wealth Ownership," 1998, based on Federal Reserve Survey of Consumer Finances. From Chuck Collins, Betsy Leonard-Wright, and Holly Sklar, "Shifting Fortunes: The Perils of the Growing American Wealth Gap," (United for a Fair Economy: 1999) p. 57.

Table A–31
Median Family Income by Age of Householder, 1947–1997 (1997 dollars)

Year	Under 25	25-34	35-44	45-54	55-64	Over 65
1947	$15,553	$19,439	$21,840	$22,815	$21,236	$12,124
1967	25,840	35,792	40,850	42,783	35,558	17,368
1973	27,251	41,506	48,650	51,765	43,461	21,851
1979	28,220	41,877	49,699	54,874	47,532	24,557
1989	22,086	39,960	52,036	59,671	48,724	29,877
1997	20,820	39,979	50,424	59,959	50,241	30,660
Annual growth rate						
1947-67	2.6%	3.1%	3.2%	3.2%	2.6%	1.8%
1967-73	0.9	2.5	3.0	3.2	3.4	3.9
1973-79	0.6	0.1	0.4	1.0	1.5	2.0
1979-89	-2.4	-0.5	0.5	0.8	0.2	2.0
1989-97	-0.7	0.0	-0.4	0.1	0.4	0.3

From "The State of Working America, 1998-99," by L. Mishel, J. Bernstein, J. Schmitt, 1999, Economic Policy Institute, p. 45. Copyright 1999 by Cornell University Press. Source: Authors' analysis of U.S. Bureau of the Census (1996) and unpublished Census data.

Table A–32
Median Family Income by Race/Ethnic Group, 1947–1997 (1997 dollars)

Year	White	Black [a]	Hispanic [b]	Ratio to white family income of: Black	Hispanic
1947	$20,938	$10,704	n.a	51.1%	n.a.
1967	36,407	21,554	n.a.	59.2	n.a.
1973	42,829	24,717	$29,635	57.7	69.2%
1979	44,330	25,103	30,731	56.6	69.3
1989	46,564	26,158	30,348	56.2	65.2
1997	46,754	28,602	28,142	61.2	60.2
Annual growth rate					
1947-67	2.8%	3.6%	n.a		
1967-73	2.7	2.3	n.a.		
1973-79	0.6	0.3	0.6%		
1979-89	0.5	0.4	-0.1		
1989-97	0.1	1.1	-0.9		

From "The State of Working America, 1998-99," by L. Mishel, J. Bernstein, J. Schmitt, 1999, Economic Policy Institute, p. 45. Copyright 1999 by Cornell University Press. Source: Authors' analysis of U.S. Bureau of the Census (1996) and unpublished Census data.

[a] Prior to 1967, data for blacks include all nonwhites.
[b] Persons of Hispanic origin may be of any race.

Table A–33
Shares of Family Income by Income Fifth and Top 5%, 1947–1997

Year	Lowest Fifth	Second Fifth	Middle Fifth	Fourth Fifth	Top Fifth	Breakdown of top fifth Bottom 15%	Top 5%	Gini Ratios
1947	5.0%	11.9%	17.0%	23.1%	43.0%	25.5%	17.5%	0.376
1967	5.4	12.2	17.5	23.5	41.4	25.0	16.4	0.358
1973	5.5	11.9	17.5	24.0	41.1	25.6	15.5	0.356
1979	5.4	11.6	17.5	24.1	41.4	26.1	15.3	0.365
1989	4.6	10.6	16.5	23.7	44.6	26.7	17.9	0.401
1997 [a]	4.2	9.9	15.7	23.0	47.2	26.5	20.7	0.429
Percentage point change								
1947-67	0.4	0.3	0.5	0.4	-1.6	-0.5	-1.1	-0.018
1967-73	0.1	-0.3	0.0	0.5	-0.3	0.6	-0.9	-0.002
1973-79	-0.1	-0.3	0.0	0.1	0.3	0.5	-0.2	0.009
1979-89	-0.8	-1.0	-1.0	-0.4	3.2	0.6	2.6	0.036
1989-97	-0.4	-0.7	-0.8	-0.7	2.6	-0.2	2.8	0.028

From "The State of Working America, 1998-99," by L. Mishel, J. Bernstein, J. Schmitt, 1999, Economic Policy Institute, p. 49. Copyright 1999 by Cornell University Press. Source: Authors' analysis of unpublished Census data.

[a] These shares reflect a change in survey methodology leading to greater inequality.

Table A–34
Ratio of Family Income of Top 5% to Lowest 20%, 1947–1997

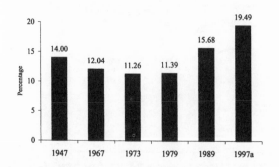

[a] This ratio reflects a change in survey methodology leading to increased inequality.

Table A–35
Real Family Income Growth by Income Group, 1947–1997, Upper Limit of Each Group (1997 dollars)

Year	Lowest Fifth	Second Fifth	Middle Fifth	Fourth Fifth	95th Percentile	Average
1947	$10,506	$16,952	$22,988	$32,618	$53,536	$23,517
1967	18,167	29,823	39,992	54,827	88,094	38,914
1973	20,678	34,120	47,606	65,468	102,063	46,321
1979	21,388	35,169	49,825	68,607	110,064	48,402
1989	20,714	36,242	52,810	77,079	128,093	53,723
1997	20,586	36,000	53,616	80,000	137,080	56,902
Annual growth rate						
1947-67	2.8%	2.9%	2.8%	2.6%	2.5%	2.5%
1967-73	2.2	2.3	2.9	3.0	2.5	2.9
1973-79	0.6	0.5	0.8	0.8	1.3	0.7
1979-89	-0.3	0.3	0.6	1.2	1.5	1.0
1989-97	-0.1	-0.1	0.2	0.5	0.9	0.7

Table A–36
Family Income, Average Annual Change

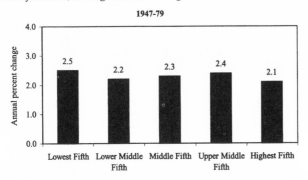

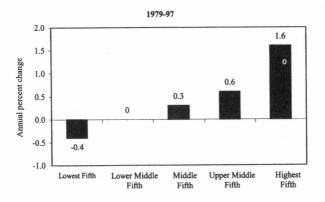

From "The State of Working America, 1998-99," by L. Mishel, J. Bernstein, J. Schmitt, 1999, Economic Policy Institute, p. 52. Copyright 1999 by Cornell University Press. Source: Authors' analysis of U.S. Bureau of the Census data (various years).

Table A–37
The Growth of Income Inequality, 1989–1996, Using Comparable Data

	Lowest Fifth	Second Fifth	Middle Fifth	Fourth Fifth	Top Fifth	80-95%	96-99%	Top 1%	Top 5%/ Bottom Fifth
Average Income									
1989	$12,745	$29,337	$45,212	$64,479	$120,203	$96,319	$164,442	$296,941	15.0
1996	12,234	28,164	44,254	64,037	125,039	97,740	177,436	326,777	17.1
Percent changes	-4.0%	-4.0%	-2.1%	-0.7%	4.0%	1.5%	7.9%	10.0%	2.0 [a]
Income Shares									*Gini ratio*
1989	5.2%	11.7%	17.1%	23.4%	42.5%	25.5%	11.6%	5.4%	0.394
1996	4.9	11.1	16.6	23.0	44.4	26.1	12.3	6.0	0.411
Point changes	-0.3	-0.7	-0.5	-0.4	1.8	0.6	0.6	0.6	0.017

From "The State of Working America, 1998-99," by L. Mishel, J. Bernstein, J. Schmitt, 1999, Economic Policy Institute, p. 55. Copyright 1999 by Cornell University Press. Source: Authors' analysis of specially constructed Current Population Survey March data.

[a] Point change.

Table A–38
Trends in Average Wages and Average Hours, 1967–1996

Year	Productivity per hour (1992=100)	Wage levels ($1997)			Hours worked		
		Annual wages	Weekly wages	Hourly wages	Annual hours	Weeks per year	Hours per week
1967	69.2	$21,830	$501.78	$12.76	1,758	43.5	39.3
1973	80.7	25,393	585.22	15.17	1,720	43.4	38.6
1979	86.3	25,580	584.02	15.05	1,745	43.8	38.8
1989	95.7	27,905	614.65	15.64	1,823	45.4	39.3
1992	100.0	27,065	597.47	15.24	1,818	45.3	39.2
1996	102.0	28,222	613.52	15.45	1,868	46.0	39.7
Annual growth rate [a]							
1967-73	2.6%	2.5%	2.6%	2.9%	-0.4%	0.0%	-0.3%
1973-79	1.1	0.1	0.0	-0.1	0.2	0.2	0.1
1979-89	1.0	0.9	0.5	0.4	0.4	0.4	0.1
1989-96	0.9	0.2	0.0	-0.2	0.3	0.2	0.1

From "The State of Working America, 1998-99," by L. Mishel, J. Bernstein, J. Schmitt, 1999, Economic Policy Institute, p. 123. Copyright 1999 by Cornell University Press. Source: Authors' analysis of Current Population Survey data and Murphy and Welch (1989).

[a] Log growth rates.

Table A-39

Growth in Private-Sector Average Hourly Wages, Benefits, and Compensation, 1987–1997 (1997 dollars)

Year [a]	Wages & Salaries	Benefits [b]	Total Compensation [c]	Benefit Share of Compensation
Hourly Pay				
1987	$15.87	$3.59	$19.46	18.4%
1988	15.59	3.64	19.23	18.9
1989	15.40	3.58	18.98	18.9
1990	15.27	3.60	18.87	19.1
1991	14.87	3.54	18.41	19.2
1992	15.05	3.62	18.67	19.4
1993	15.08	3.62	18.69	19.3
1994	14.93	3.68	18.62	19.8
1995	14.64	3.46	18.10	19.1
1996	14.62	3.37	17.99	18.8
1997	14.72	3.26	17.98	18.1
Change 1989-97				
Dollars	-$1.15	-$0.33	-$1.48	
Percent	-7.3%	-9.2%	-7.6%	

From "The State of Working America, 1998-99," by L. Mishel, J. Bernstein, J. Schmitt, 1999, Economic Policy Institute, p. 126. Copyright 1999 by Cornell University Press. Source: Authors' analysis of BLS ECI levels data.

[a] Data are for March.
[b] Includes payroll taxes, health, pension, and other nonwage benefits.
[c] Deflated by CPI-U-X1, except health deflated by CPI-U-X1 medical care index.

Table A-40

Wages for All Workers by Wage Percentile, 1973–1997

Year	Wage by percentile [a]								
	10	20	30	40	50	60	70	80	90
Real hourly wage ($1997)									
1973	$6.07	$7.33	$8.70	$10.13	$11.61	$13.32	$15.46	$17.68	$22.22
1979	6.42	7.33	8.61	10.13	11.46	13.27	15.69	18.29	22.46
1989	5.39	6.71	8.05	9.62	11.18	13.05	15.53	18.57	23.46
1992	5.49	6.68	7.99	9.34	11.16	12.75	15.10	18.24	23.07
1997	5.46	6.74	7.94	9.25	10.82	12.69	15.08	18.37	23.90

From "The State of Working America, 1998-99," by L. Mishel, J. Bernstein, J. Schmitt, 1999, Economic Policy Institute, p. 131. Copyright 1999 by Cornell University Press. Source: Authors' analysis.

[a] Wage at which x% of the wage earners earn less and (100-x)% earn more.

Table A–41
Wages for Male and Female Workers by Wage Percentile, 1973–1997

Year	Wage by percentile [a]								
	10	20	30	40	50	60	70	80	90
Real hourly wage ($1997)									
Male workers									
1973	$7.16	$9.19	$10.84	12.42	$14.08	$15.96	$17.56	$20.21	$25.74
1979	7.07	8.98	10.80	12.56	14.39	16.33	18.32	21.27	25.93
1989	6.17	7.73	9.49	11.23	13.07	15.38	17.79	20.85	26.12
1992	5.79	7.31	9.02	10.81	12.54	14.63	17.22	20.44	26.16
1997	5.92	7.36	8.86	10.29	12.19	14.44	17.02	20.18	26.44
Real hourly wage ($1997)									
Female workers									
1973	$5.05	$6.27	$7.05	$7.89	$8.89	$10.01	$11.27	$13.00	$16.07
1979	6.13	6.64	7.22	8.05	9.03	10.27	11.46	13.32	16.62
1989	5.02	6.18	7.15	8.22	9.55	10.91	12.85	15.40	19.33
1992	5.20	6.06	7.13	8.35	9.55	11.21	12.82	15.50	20.00
1997	5.15	6.14	7.16	8.25	9.63	11.08	13.07	15.91	20.61

From "The State of Working America, 1998-99," by L. Mishel, J. Bernstein, J. Schmitt, 1999, Economic Policy Institute, p. 132-3. Copyright 1999 by Cornell University Press. Source: Authors' analysis.

[a] Wage at which x% of wage earners earn less and (100-x)% earn more.

Table A–42
Changes in the Gender Wage Differential, 1973–1997

Year	Median hourly wage ($1997)			Women's share of employment
	Male	Female	Ratio	
1973	$14.08	$8.89	63.1%	38.5%
1979	14.39	9.03	62.8	41.7
1989	13.07	9.55	73.1	45.2
1997	12.19	9.63	79.0	46.2
1989 (alt.)[a]	14.39	9.55	66.4	
1997 (alt.)[a]	14.39	9.63	66.9	
Change				
1979-89	-$1.32	$0.52	10.3	
1989-97	-0.88	0.08	5.9	

Contribution to narrowing of gender wage gap: [b]

Period	Male wage decline	Female wage growth	Total
1979-89	64.9%	35.1%	100.0%
1989-97	74.4	25.6	100.0

From "The State of Working America, 1998-99," by L. Mishel, J. Bernstein, J. Schmitt, 1999, Economic Policy Institute, p. 135. Copyright 1999 by Cornell University Press. Source: Authors' analysis.

[a] Alternative scenario if male wages did not decline in real terms since 1979.
[b] The contribution of "female wage growth" is the growth of the gender differential assuming male real wages did not fall (the alternative scenario), relative to the actual change in the differential.

Table A-43

Share of All Workers Earning Poverty Level Hourly Wages and Multiples, 1973–1997

| | Share of employment by wage multiple of poverty wage [a] | | | | | | | |
| | Poverty level wages: | | | | | | | |
Year	0-75	75-100	Total [b]	100-125	125-200	200-300	300+	Total
Total								
1973	8.0%	15.6%	23.5%	13.3%	34.7%	19.9%	8.6%	100.0%
1979	4.2	19.4	23.7	15.3	31.4	21.0	8.7	100.0
1989	13.4	15.1	28.5	13.5	29.2	19.1	9.7	100.0
1997	12.1	16.5	28.6	14.1	29.6	17.3	10.3	100.0
Change								
1973-79	-3.7	3.9	0.1	2.0	-3.3	1.1	0.0	
1979-89	9.2	-4.3	4.9	-1.8	-2.2	-1.9	1.0	
1989-97	-1.3	1.3	0.1	0.6	0.4	-1.7	0.7	
Men								
1973	3.8%	9.0%	12.8%	9.7%	36.7%	27.9%	12.9%	100.0%
1979	2.4	11.0	13.4	11.3	32.1	29.6	13.6	100.0
1989	9.1	12.1	21.2	11.3	29.7	23.7	14.1	100.0
1997	8.8	13.7	22.5	12.6	30.6	20.5	13.8	100.0
Change								
1973-79	-1.5	2.1	0.6	1.6	-4.6	1.7	0.6	
1979-89	6.8	1.1	7.8	0.0	-2.5	-5.9	0.5	
1989-97	-0.3	1.6	1.3	1.3	0.9	-3.2	-0.3	
Women								
1973	14.0%	25.1%	39.1%	18.6%	31.7%	8.3%	2.3%	100.0%
1979	6.7	30.4	37.0	20.5	30.4	9.8	2.3	100.0
1989	18.2	18.6	36.8	16.0	28.6	13.8	4.7	100.0
1997	15.7	19.5	35.3	15.8	28.5	13.9	6.6	100.0
Change								
1973-79	-7.3	5.3	-2.1	1.9	-1.2	1.5	0.0	
1979-89	11.6	-11.8	-0.3	-4.5	-1.8	4.1	2.5	
1989-97	-2.5	1.0	-1.5	-0.3	-0.1	0.0	1.8	

From "The State of Working America, 1998-99," by L. Mishel, J. Bernstein, J. Schmitt, 1999, Economic Policy Institute, p. 136. Copyright 1999 by Cornell University Press. Source: Authors' analysis.

[a] The wage ranges are equivalent in 1996 dollars to: $5.78 and below (0-75), $5.79-$7.71(75-100), $7.72-$9.64 (100-125), $9.65-$15.42 (125-200), $15.43-$23.13 (200-300), and $23.14 and above (300+).
[b] Combines lowest two categories and represents the share of wage earners earning poverty-level wages.

Table A–44
Share of Workers Earning Poverty-Level Wages, by Race/Ethnicity, 1973–1997

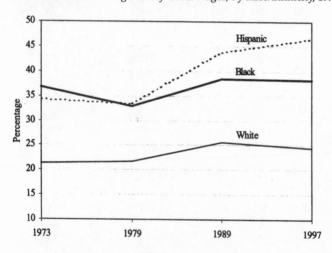

Table A–45

Share of Workers Earning Poverty Level Hourly Wages and Multiples, by Race/ Ethnicity, 1973–1997

	Share of employment by wage multiple of poverty wage [a]							
	Poverty level wages:							
Year	0-75	75-100	Total [b]	100-125	125-200	200-300	300+	Total
Whites								
1973	6.9%	14.4%	21.3%	12.9%	35.0%	21.2%	9.5%	100%
1979	3.9	17.9	21.8	14.8	31.8	22.1	9.6	100.0
1989	11.9	13.8	25.6	13.1	29.8	20.5	10.9	100.0
1997	10.0	14.4	24.5	13.5	30.8	19.3	12.0	100.0
Change	-3.0	3.5	0.5	1.8	-3.2	0.9	0.0	
1973-79	8.0	-4.2	3.8	-1.6	-1.9	-1.6	1.4	
1979-89	-1.8	0.7	-1.2	0.3	1.0	-1.2	1.1	
1989-97								
Blacks								
1973	14.8%	22.0%	36.8%	14.8%	32.9%	12.3%	3.2%	100.0%
1979	6.3	26.5	32.8	17.9	29.9	15.7	3.8	100.0
1989	19.1	19.4	38.5	15.7	27.0	14.4	4.3	100.0
1997	16.3	21.9	38.2	17.2	28.1	12.0	4.6	100.0
Change								
1973-79	-8.5	4.5	-4.0	3.0	-3.0	3.4	0.6	
1979-89	12.8	-7.1	5.7	-2.2	-2.9	-1.2	0.6	
1989-97	-2.8	2.5	-0.3	1.5	1.0	-2.4	0.2	
Hispanics								
1973	12.2%	22.2%	34.3%	16.8%	34.1%	11.5%	3.2%	100.0%
1979	5.3	28.2	33.5	18.0	29.8	14.8	3.8	100.0
1989	20.9	22.9	43.8	14.7	26.1	11.6	3.9	100.0
1997	21.9	24.8	46.7	15.8	24.0	9.4	4.0	100.0
Change								
1973-79	-6.8	6.0	-0.8	0.0	-4.3	3.3	0.6	
1979-89	15.5	-5.2	10.3	-3.4	-3.8	-3.2	0.0	
1989-97	1.0	1.9	2.9	1.2	-2.1	-2.2	0.2	

From "The State of Working America, 1998-99," by L. Mishel, J. Bernstein, J. Schmitt, 1999, Economic Policy Institute, p. 140-2. Copyright 1999 by Cornell University Press. Source: Authors' analysis.

[a] The wage ranges are equivalent in 1996 dollars to: $5.78 and below (0-75), $5.79-$7.71(75-100), $7.72-$9.64 (100-125), $9.65-$15.42 (125-200), $15.43-$23.13 (200-300), and $23.14 and above (300+).
[b] Combines lowest two categories and represents the share of wage earners earning poverty-level wages.

Appendix B: Family Assistance Plan, Negative Income Tax, Guaranteed Income

In the 1960s, an idea called a negative income tax, promoted by economists such as Milton Friedman, James Tobin, and Robert Lampman, gained currency in academic circles. The concept seemed simple: people with less than specified income (i.e., poor people) would report their income to IRS, which would credit money to them in accordance with an income scale. The benefit would be used first to defray any tax due from them. Any remainder would be paid to them as a tax refund.

In theory, a basic income would be guaranteed to the poor—thus the name "guaranteed income"—but government payments would decline as the income that recipients received from earnings rose. Payments would be scaled so that earning an income would always be more advantageous to recipients, that is, they would be provided with an incentive to work.

Simple in concept and thought to be simple in administration, the program would replace AFDC and other welfare programs.

The idea seemed eminently desirable to prominent newspapers and to many citizens. President Lyndon Johnson established a National Commission on Income Maintenance Programs to study welfare issues, and commission members presented him with a recommendation favoring a negative income tax. However, he never acted on the recommendation.

In August 1969, President Richard Nixon introduced legislation along similar lines that would establish a Family Assistance Plan (FAP). The proposal dominated the debate about welfare well into the 1970s. As Congress held hearings and protagonists and opponents had their say, however, it turned out that FAP would be much more difficult in practice than anyone had imagined.

"Family" had to be defined—married parents or unmarried? One parent or two parents? It appeared that the "guarantee" would be either desperately low or would add unacceptable numbers of people to the welfare rolls. Even the guaranteed income that the president introduced—$1,600 a year, a low figure even at that time—would have doubled the number of people receiving assistance. And would it really provide an incentive to work or would some people, satisfied to live on $1,600, never work?

In the end, Congress voted down a bill that was several hundred pages long and AFDC remained on the books. However, a comparatively simple program for the aged and disabled, administered by the Social Security Administration, was enacted as a result of the debate. It replaced older, more unwieldy programs that had been administered by public assistance agencies. Legislation for the aged and disabled had not aroused the same kind of controversy about incentive to work and morality as the proposal to replace AFDC.

Although there are important differences, it may also be said that the negative income tax is the model on which the current Earned Income Tax Credit is based.

A blow-by-blow account of the struggle over FAP may be found in a book called *Nixon's Good Deed, Welfare Reform*, by Vincent J. and Vee Burke, published by Columbia University Press in in 1974. An early debate abut the underlying concept may be found in James

Tobin, "The Case for an Income Guarantee." *The Public Interest* no. 4, Summer 1966, in Alvin L. Schorr, "Against a Negative Income Tax," and in James Tobin, "A Rejoinder," *The Public Interest*, no. 5, Fall 1966.

Appendix C: Medicare for Children (Kiddiecare)

OUTLINE OF SPECIFICATIONS

1. All children through the age of eighteen and all pregnant women would be covered for the full range of services they may need, including dental care and well baby and preventive care in particular.

2. All children under the age of eighteen would automatically be eligible for coverage. Women who can establish that they are pregnant also would be automatically eligible.

3. Patients would seek and receive such care through the physician, neighborhood clinic, community health center, Preferred Provider Organization, or HMO of their choice.

4. Children's families would pay modest deductibles and 20 percent of covered charges, as in Medicare, *except that* payments would be waived for any member of a family that had received Unemployment Insurance, food stamps, TANF, or Medicaid within the prior two years.

5. Alternative financing mechanisms include adding a small increment to the Medicare payroll tax, to patients' payment of deductibles or cost sharing, an increment to "sin" taxes, recapturing money that would be saved by Medicaid or other public programs, and general revenue funds.

6. If it appears desirable that the program build up slowly, it is feasible to embark on it in stages; for example, by beginning with children under six years of age and moving two years of age upward every year.

7. The program would be administered by arrangement between a quasi-public board and the Social Security Administration. Regional boards with appointed consumer and professional representatives would monitor service delivery.

Selected Readings

There has been an outpouring of literature about welfare reform since shortly after it was enacted in 1996. The following books and series of reports are among those that appear to offer dependable perspective on what was happening and where welfare reform came from.

Winifred Bell. *Aid to Dependent Children*. New York: Columbia University Press, 1965. A classic study of the dynamics of policy development in ADC forty years ago.

Center on Budget and Policy Priorities. Washington, D.C., 20002. A regular series of reports on poverty, income distribution, wages, medical care, and TANF. For example, *Poverty and Income Trends: 1998*. Reliable and knowledgeable.

Blanche D. Coll. *Safety Net: Welfare and Social Security, 1929–1979*. New Brunswick, NJ: Rutgers University Press, 1995. A detailed account of the recent history of welfare by one who worked in the federal program during much of the period she describes.

Kathryn Edin and Laura Lein. *Making Ends Meet: How Single Mothers Survive Welfare and Low-Wage Work*. New York: Russell Sage, 1997. A careful report of the daily lives of what the authors call "welfare reliant" and "wage reliant" poor mothers, stressing the similarities between the two groups.

Martin Gilens. *Why Americans Hate Welfare: Race, Media and the Politics of Antipoverty Policy*. Chicago: University of Chicago Press, 1999. A subtly reasoned book, drawing extensively on survey data, to arrive at the reasons for American attitudes to welfare.

Linda Gordon. *Pitied but Not Entitled—Single Mothers and the History of Welfare, 1890–1935*. New York: The Free Press, 1994. A thoughtful history of the background of welfare, bringing its development more up to date than the subtitle suggests.

Manpower Demonstration Research Corporation. An extensive series of evaluation reports, reporting findings of studies of welfare reform programs in states and localities. For example, Virginia Knox, Cynthia Miller, and Lisa A. Gennetian. *Reforming Welfare and Rewarding Work*, Volume 1: *Effects on Adults* and Volume 2: *Effects on Children*. New York: Manpower Demonstration Research Corporation, August 2000, a report on Minnesota's Family Investment Program.

Lawrence Mishel, Jared Bernstein and John Schmitt. *The State of Working America, 1998–99*. Ithaca, NY: Economic Policy Institute, Cornell University Press, 1999. An examination of the impact of the economy on the living standards of Americans. Packed with data.

Katherine S. Newman. *No Shame in My Game: The Working Poor in the Inner City*. New York: Russell Sage Foundation/Knopf, 1998. Based on interviews with over 300 working poor families in black and Puerto Rican neighborhoods in New York, Newman provides a vivid picture of the daily lives of the working poor and an acute analysis of their situation.

Bruce Nissen, ed. *U.S. Labor Relations, Accommodation and Conflict, 1945–1989.* New York and London: Garland Publishing, 1990. A thoughtful set of essays about post-WWII industrial relations.

U.S. House of Representatives, Ways and Means Committee. *1998 Green Book.* Washington, DC: U.S. Government Printing Office, 1999. An authoritative description of AFDC and TANF, with full program data and reports of studies on the programs.

The Urban Institute. *Assessing the New Federalism.* Washington, DC. Occasional papers, relying on a household survey and studies of policy in thirteen states, that assess the devolution of responsibility for social programs, including TANF, to states. For example, number 37, *Making Sure Where We Started: State Employment and Training Systems for Welfare Recipients on the Eve of Federal Welfare Reform.* Also a series of papers presenting findings from the National Survey of America's Families. For example, Pamela Loprest, "How Families that Left Welfare Are Doing," August 1999. Reliable data and knowledgeable analysis.

Chaim I. Waxman. *The Stigma of Poverty.* New York: Pergamon Press, 1983. A critique of poverty theories and policies.

Index

About the Author

ALVIN L. SCHORR is Leonard W. Mayo Professor of Family and Child Welfare Emeritus, Mandel School of Applied Social Sciences, Case Western Reserve University. During Professor Schorr's long, distinguished career he has served as Dean of the New York University School of Social Work, Deputy Assistant Secretary, U.S. Department of Health, Education and Welfare, and Director of Long Range Research, U.S. Social Security Administration. He has published seven earlier books on social policies.